How to Conduct Survey Research:
A Guide for Schools

Alicia Williams
Nancy Protheroe

Because research and information make the difference.

Educational Research Service
1001 North Fairfax Street, Suite 500 • Alexandria, VA 22314-1587
Phone: 703-243-2100 • Toll Free: 800-791-9308
Fax: 703-243-1985 • Toll Free: 800-791-9309
Email: ers@ers.org • Web site: www.ers.org

Educational Research Service is the nonprofit organization serving the research and information needs of the nation's preK-12 education leaders and the public. Founded by the national school management associations, ERS provides quality, objective research and information that enable education leaders to make the most effective school decisions in both day-to-day operations and long-range planning. Refer to the end of this book for information on the benefits of an annual ERS subscription, and for an order form listing resources that complement this book. Or visit us online at www.ers.org for an overview of available resources.

ERS e-Knowledge Portal
http://portal.ers.org

ERS Founding Organizations:
American Association of School Administrators
American Association of School Personnel Administrators
Association of School Business Officials International
National Association of Elementary School Principals
National Association of Secondary School Principals
National School Public Relations Association

ERS Executive Staff:
Katherine A. Behrens, Acting President and Chief Operating Officer
Kathleen McLane, Chief Knowledge Officer

Library of Congress Cataloging-in-Publication Data
Williams, Alicia R. (Alicia Renee).
How to conduct survey research : a guide for schools / Alicia Williams and Nancy Protheroe.
      p. cm.
Includes bibliographical references.
ISBN 978-1-931762-69-4
      1. Educational surveys–Handbooks, manuals, etc. 2. Education–Research–Handbooks, manuals, etc. I. Protheroe, Nancy. II. Title.

LB2823.W497 2008
370.7'2–dc22   2008006640

Authors: Alicia Williams and Nancy Protheroe
Editor: Tracy Pastian
Layout & Design: Susie McKinley and Libby McNulty

Ordering Information: Additional copies of this publication may be purchased at the base price of $28.00; ERS School District Subscriber: $14.00; ERS Individual Subscriber: $21.00. Quantity discounts available. Add the greater of $4.50 or 10% of total purchase price for shipping and handling. Phone orders accepted with Visa, MasterCard, or American Express. Stock No. 0711. ISBN 978-1-931762-69-4.

Note: ERS is solely responsible for this publication; no approval or endorsement by ERS founders is implied.

Table of Contents

Foreword

School district leaders frequently need to gather information about the opinions and perceptions of parents, community members, and others with an interest in the school system. There are many popular methods for gathering anecdotal information informally, such as community meetings, PTA gatherings, etc. However, gathering useful information that will be valid and reliable usually calls for conducting a survey. This may seem intimidating, but it does not need to be. Given the role that ERS has in conducting nationwide, annual surveys, we are frequently contacted by administrators and other school leaders with questions about their own survey needs. Their questions are the foundation of this guide.

The goal of this book is to take the mystery out of the survey process by providing readable, practical information that will help school leaders plan and conduct surveys that yield usable data—and communicate the data in a way that will truly benefit the district decision-making process. This guide was originally developed by Alicia Williams, our former Director of Survey Research, and completed by Nancy Protheroe, our Director of Special Research Projects.

We welcome your feedback and your suggestions. Let us know how we can help you.

Kathleen McLane
Chief Knowledge Officer
Educational Research Service

Chapter 1

What Can a Survey Do for Me?

A district's central office leadership team and school board are considering the possibility of reconfiguring several of the district's schools in light of declining enrollment and limited resources. Prior to making any decisions, however, the leadership team intends to communicate several proposed scenarios to residents, parents, and staff members, then ask about their views concerning each proposal.

A high school principal is interested in asking recent graduates how well they feel the school prepared them for transitioning into higher education or the work world. She intends to use this information to help pinpoint areas in need of improvement.

The business manager of a small school district wrestles with the issue of how to meet the needs of its students with regard to improving instructional technology, increasing classroom space, and making needed building repairs. It is clear that the district will need to allocate substantial funds to address these needs in the next several years; however, the estimated cost is far more than the district's operating budget or building reserves can cover. After talking with the superintendent and school board, the decision is made to consider including a bond referendum in the next election. Since a bond referendum 3 years before had been defeated, the district leadership decides to first gather information from the community about what types of projects people are most likely to support, as well as reasons given for why a referendum might not be supported. This information will be used to craft a marketing campaign intended to address community concerns and build support before the referendum.

An assistant principal of an elementary school has been tasked with the job of collecting information from parents concerning their views of the school's instructional program, as well as attitudes about its physical environment and school safety issues. The data collected will be used to inform staff and parents working on school improvement planning and to identify areas about which the school might need to do a better job communicating with parents.

These are just a few examples of how education leaders are increasingly relying on surveys to gather needed information from key stakeholders. Surveys are used, for example, to assess community attitudes regarding bond referenda, inform decisions about instructional programs, and pinpoint areas for school improvement. Collecting survey data has become especially important for schools in these times of shifting community demographics, policy shifts toward increased accountability, and sometimes heated debates about education goals.

Consider this example. Respondents to one district's survey generally placed high priority on high-cost programs, such as decreasing class size or markedly increasing teachers' salaries. However, they also indicated that an increase in school taxes "would be unwise at this time," and decisions to implement the high-cost programs should be considered with special care. What at first looked like a program with popular support could turn into a highly charged and negative issue if additional funds to pay for it are required.

In this case, school decision makers were provided not only with information about their community's priorities for the schools, but they were also given insight into potential public relations and funding problems. Since school improvement often involves a complex array of problems, knowledge of political and economic realities are frequently crucial to the success of a new program or acceptance of a decision. A well-constructed needs assessment survey should provide data on a variety of relevant issues.

In addition, surveys should be considered more than simply data collection tools. Bedrosian and Kritch talk about this. In their view, a survey can act as "an excellent vehicle for promoting discussion and understanding in the community... [and] a catalyst for greater community involvement in the decision making process" (1990, p. 39). The survey process demonstrates to community members that their opinions are valued.

Because surveys can identify problems and opportunities while simultaneously developing public support, they can be extremely valuable and cost-effective tools for school leaders. To get the best value from a survey, however, careful attention must be paid to the technical aspects of the project.

Conducting survey research may seem simple—after all, it is only a matter of asking questions—but carrying out a survey that yields useful and reliable information takes planning, careful consideration, and knowledge of technical aspects. However, it can be done well if people working on the project take the time to educate themselves and to carefully plan all aspects of the project. Attention to detail is a key determinant of whether a survey yields "good" data.

This guide has been designed to provide school leaders with easy-to-use, practical information on planning and conducting surveys. The topics follow the typical sequence of the survey process: establishing the goals of your survey, selecting prospective participants, estimating the sample size, choosing a method for survey delivery, developing a budget and timeline for the project, developing and testing the survey instrument, administering the survey, reviewing the data, and analyzing and sharing the results. Suggestions for ways to avoid common pitfalls are also included.

The Big Picture

It is sometimes tempting to jump right into the details of a survey project, such as immediately developing questions to ask or identifying who to survey, but taking a more global approach is almost always more productive. By stepping back and looking at the process as a whole, you are likely to have a better grasp of what the project might require in terms of time, finances, and staff involvement. Figure 1.1 defines some of the major steps needed in most survey projects.

Figure 1.1. Survey Process Chart

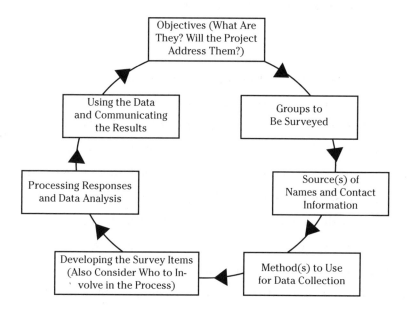

The graphic depiction of a survey project can be helpful in another way. Planning a survey is often a recursive process—you go back and forth among the planning of different tasks and functions as you find, for instance, that a fairly immediate need for data might suggest that there is not enough time for a mailed survey. Thus, a decision may need to be made to either abandon the project altogether or take a different approach to collecting data.

By stepping back and taking a big picture look—asking some preliminary questions about what will need to be done to address different tasks on the cycle—you are more likely to have a realistic framework within which you can plan your project.

Notes:_____

_____

_____

_____

_____

_____

_____

_____

_____

_____

_____

_____

_____

_____

_____

_____

_____

_____

_____

_____

_____

_____

_____

_____

_____

_____

_____

_____

_____

_____

Notes:_____

_____

_____

_____

_____

_____

_____

_____

_____

_____

_____

_____

_____

_____

_____

_____

_____

_____

_____

_____

_____

_____

_____

_____

_____

_____

_____

_____

Chapter 2

Determining Your Purpose and Population

> "Would you tell me, please, which way I ought to go from here?" (Alice to the Cheshire Cat)
> "That depends a great deal on where you want to get to," said the cat.
> *Alice in Wonderland* by Lewis Carroll

Step 1. Establish the Goals and Objectives of Your Survey

In his book, *The Seven Habits of Highly Effective People*, Steven Covey included "Begin with the end in mind" as one of the critical habits (1990). Educators across the country have also been introduced to the phrase through their use of the instructional planning process developed by Grant Wiggins and Jay McTighe (1998). Both the phrase and the approach are significant to the process of planning a survey project that will generate relevant data in a cost-effective manner.

Too many survey projects begin with the general notion that "it would be a good idea to..." or that "it's time to do another ..." Often, this approach produces a hodgepodge of questions and data that are never put to productive use. Don't fall into that trap.

Instead, begin with the end in mind. Think about the "big" questions you want answered and how you plan to use the data that are gathered. Use that knowledge to guide you along the way as you develop questions, identify the groups to be surveyed, and select a way to get the survey to these people.

Objectives may be broad or very specific in scope. Listed below are some general objectives established by actual school districts as they developed their needs assessments:

- to assess the status of and to improve school communications with the community

- to evaluate the foreign language program in the district's secondary schools from the standpoint of students' needs

- to determine the extent to which both the general public and parents of elementary-age children perceive the schools as meeting their needs

- to compare residents' priorities for district programs with priorities measured on the national level by the Annual Gallup Poll of the Public's Attitudes Toward the Public Schools

Most problems with surveys stem from project objectives that are unclear or are trying to achieve too many things. Avoid such problems by setting clear, explicit expectations for what the project is intended to do. Use the objectives as a guideline at every step along the way. For example, repeatedly ask yourself during the questionnaire design phase—is this question, although it might be interesting, really necessary to address our survey objective?

Consider the problems that can arise when objectives are not made explicit. A school district is considering the initiation of after-school programs. It was assumed, but not made explicit, during the planning phase that responses of parents with children in school would be considered as a special group. Survey instruments were sent to a random sample of residents, but the instrument did not include an item that asked respondents whether they had children in school. One objective of the study—to assess the needs of parents of children in school—could not be met, since it was not made explicit and the survey instrument provided no way to separate this specific group from other respondents.

There is another advantage to making objectives explicit—it is clear what the project is *not* intended to address. For example, if the objective clearly states that the data collected will focus on academic programs at the elementary school level, there will be no anticipation that the needs assessment will generate information needed for decisions about high school extracurricular activities.

There are two additional guidelines you should keep in mind when developing both your "big picture" and the specific objectives for a survey project:

- If you intend to use the data only if the results support a particular proposal, don't conduct the survey. To do so and suppress the results leads to a loss of credibility and trust—implications far broader than the survey project.

- If you don't want to know the answer, don't ask the question. There may be times when school leaders need to make a difficult decision—and already know what that decision must be. Asking for

community input that might point to another alternative would serve only to increase resistance
and dissatisfaction.

The underlying purpose of a survey project should be the collection of data to use in making decisions. Collecting data with the intent of ignoring it if the results are counter to the responses you desire is not only expensive and deceptive—it can also result in a public relations nightmare. As soon as the survey is distributed—by mail, by phone, or in person—people are aware that an issue is being studied and there is interest in the results. Moreover, the survey results are news, with the possibility that it may become embarrassing if the results are ignored or suppressed.

For example, suppose that an increase in revenues available to the district will permit the hiring of additional teachers to reduce class size. After studying the research on class size, the superintendent decides to recommend to the board that the funds be used to decrease class size in grades one through three.

During a school board meeting, a proposal is made to survey residents and teachers as to whether their preference is for decreasing class size in the first three grades or for decreasing class size in grades K through 12. At first glance, this might seem a good idea from the standpoint of public relations. But what if the across-the-board decrease option receives the most support even though respondents have been told in the survey instrument that an across-the-board reduction will result in an average decrease of only one pupil per class? District administrators and board members will be faced with a dilemma: Either implement a plan that research says will not improve student achievement or go ahead with the recommended plan against the expressed views of the public.

Questions to Consider Before You Start:
- What do you want to know?
- Who do you need to ask?
- How will the information be used?

At this stage of the survey project, it is especially important to gather opinions about what issues and questions the survey instrument should address—and then communicate the decided-on objectives to the people whose opinions were solicited. Since a single survey cannot possibly address all desired questions, the planning may involve difficult decisions. However, facing these decisions now will avoid disappointment down the road.

Once you have clearly defined the objectives of your survey, consider whether there are existing archival data available that may answer some of the questions of interest. For instance, a survey conducted for your school in the recent past may have asked questions similar to those being considered. Are the data from that project really too old to be of use? If there are data that are already available on a particular issue or topic relevant to your survey, make sure there is a compelling reason to ask those questions again in your new survey. A survey project—in particular the design of the survey instrument—involves a constant balancing of costs against benefits.

Some of these costs are financial, since longer surveys or surveys sent to more people will be more expensive. Another cost involves the quality of the data collected. A higher response rate will give you more confidence in the data collected, and a longer survey, perhaps one that includes "nice to ask" but not essential questions, may decrease your response rate. More will be discussed on this topic later, but, in the meantime, keep this in mind: Prospective respondents generally do not like surveys with too many questions.

Some final considerations relating to the development of objectives: Are they achievable? Do they lend themselves to a solution—a decision—that will be enhanced by the use of data from the survey? If not, further work should focus on the objectives before proceeding. Be realistic

---

Some Common Characteristics of Surveys

Although surveys come in many different forms and serve a wide variety of purposes, they typically have some common characteristics, regardless of their purpose:

- Although they generally gather information from only a small sample of people (unless a census approach is used), their intent is to provide a representative profile of the population from which the sample was drawn.
- The sample is generally selected so that each individual in the population has a known chance of selection.
- Information is collected by means of standardized questions so that everyone surveyed responds to exactly the same questions.
- Answers from individual respondents generally are not identified. Instead, survey results are presented in the aggregate—typically in the form of tables, charts, and graphs.

---

about what can be "solved" with data from a survey. An objective that is overly general or ambitious can result in frustration and a lower level of quality than might have been obtained if the plan had been realistic.

Step 2. Select Survey Participants

Once you have established the objectives for your survey, you will need to make some decisions about who will be surveyed. For instance, a school climate survey would be appropriate for people with some involvement with the school (e.g., students, parents, teachers) but not for community residents with little to no contact with it.

Another consideration at this step is the availability of a data file with contact information about the types of people you would like to survey. For example, you might be especially interested in the opinions of people who voted against a previous bond referendum, but there is no database of names of people voting "no." In this case, you might need to use responses to survey items in addition to an only partially "good enough" database to gather the data you need. For example, the survey could be sent to a sample of registered voters, with respondents asked to indicate whether they voted in the bond referendum election and whether they voted to support or reject the referendum. Responses from the group as a whole could be split into several groups, one of which would be people who voted to reject the previous referendum.

This example also highlights something that was mentioned before—specifically, the recursive nature of survey

Figure 2.1. The Survey Project:
Taking a Big Picture Approach

Use this form to help you begin thinking about your survey project. Your answers should be brief but as specific as possible. Also, realize that some of your answers/plans may need to change as you address another question and find, for example, that financial or staff resources you anticipate needing for a particular approach will not be available. Being flexible—and realistic—in this "thinking about" exercise helps set the stage for productive planning.

Objectives: Why are we conducting the survey? What questions do we need answered? _____

_____

_____

_____

_____

When is the data needed? _____

Costs and Resources: What are some anticipated costs? What will be available to support the project in terms of funding, staff time, and/or outside help? _____

_____

_____

_____

_____

Group(s) to Be Surveyed: Who will have the information we need? Whose opinions are important to the issue being discussed? Is there a source for these names, addresses, etc.? _____

_____

_____

_____

_____

Method to Be Used for Data Collection: Mailed survey, web-based, telephone interview, etc.? Combination of methods? How long is it likely to take to collect data this way? What resources (financial, staff, etc.) will be needed to take this approach? _____

_____

_____

_____

_____

Who should be involved in planning? (Might be different people for different aspects of planning.) _____

_____

_____

_____

_____

Questions/Information to Address on the Survey Instrument: What are key items that should be included in the survey instrument? Be sure these will help address project objectives. However, don't be concerned with the exact wording. _____

_____

_____

_____

_____

Reality Check: Are there aspects of the survey process identified here that will not fit together? (For example, not enough time to collect data through a mailed survey to meet the date by which data is needed.) What could be changed to make successful completion of the survey project more likely? _____

_____

_____

_____

_____

_____

project planning. A list of people voting "no" is not available. Obviously, you would not want to waste resources on sending the survey to "yes" people and then not using their responses. Instead, you might design survey items that help determine why the "yes" people voted that way, and then use the information to inform your strategy during the current election.

This brings up another point that will be discussed in more detail later. If the project objectives point to the importance of knowing about the responses of subgroups of people, a larger sample size will be needed since each of these smaller groups, in essence, represents its own population. For the time being, however, plan on focusing on responses of subgroups of respondents only if such data is essential to meeting project objectives.

Understanding Sampling

An aspect of needs assessment surveys that requires special attention is design of the sampling procedures to be used. Although the ideal approach might be to contact everyone in the community or the entire teaching staff of the district for their opinions about what the schools should be doing, often this is not practical. Instead, we select a part of that group (called a sample), study the opinions and attitudes of the sample, and then use that information to make generalizations about the larger group (the population).

When designing a survey project or reporting the data, a question sometimes asked is: Are sample data really accurate? Although it is possible for sample data to misrepresent the population, careful attention to sampling procedures and thoughtful interpretation of results at the data analysis and reporting stages will minimize this possibility. Use of sample data is statistically appropriate and, in most cases, a more efficient expenditure of district resources.

> The objective of sampling is to select
> a group (sample) that is representative
> of the population.

A particular value of the population, such as average income or level of education, is called a *parameter*. Its counterpart in the sample, is called a *statistic*. We can estimate parameters in the population by using corresponding statistics in the sample, if we use care in selecting a random sample of the population. Three aspects of this problem that must be addressed include: 1) defining the population, 2) selecting a sampling strategy, and 3) determining the size of the sample.

To some extent, sampling theory provides answers to these questions, but developing a thorough understanding of the objectives for the needs assessment survey as well as the limitations placed on it is just as important. The "best" sample design for one school district may fail to collect the information needed by another district. Or, it may be too expensive or too time-consuming. The sampling approach used must be practical and designed to yield the desired information.

Defining the Population

A population is the total group about whom information is desired, a decision made based on the objectives of the survey. The population may be the entire community or teachers or recent graduates from the district. A sampling unit is a member of this population and the sampling frame is the "master list" from which the members of the sample are drawn. Although a random sample will be truly representative only if all members of the universe are included on the list and if each has an equal chance of being selected, the sampling frame may sometimes unavoidably fail to include all possible sampling units. It should, however, be a reasonable facsimile of the population that it is intended to represent.

In the example below, a roster of PTA members would be inappropriate for use as a sampling frame if information were desired about the attitudes of the community in general. However, the roster could be used if the universe specified in the objective happened to be PTA members. If there were no recent census addresses available, the voter registration list—even though eliminating all who had not registered to vote—might be a necessary, although far from ideal, alternative.

OBJECTIVE: To assess the attitudes of the community toward school programs:

✗ Roster of PTA members — No.
○ Voter registration list — Maybe.
✔ Addresses from recent district census — Yes.

Census Versus Sample

When one hears the word "census," what typically comes to mind is the federal census conducted every 10 years by the U.S. Census Bureau. A census, in fact, is any survey which asks *every* member of the population of interest to participate. In the case of the federal census, the United States government attempts to gather demographic and housing data on everyone residing in the United States. In a school census, all teachers and students may be asked to participate in the survey.

In terms of the precision of the results, a census is the best method to use for gathering information about a population of interest. If you want to know a population's precise beliefs, perceptions, experiences, personal and educational background, and so forth, ask all the members directly. A census eliminates any concerns about sampling errors (i.e., the degree to which results may differ from the true population because of the way in which the sample was selected) because all members of the population of interest are being surveyed. However, a census can be extremely costly and labor-intensive if the population is large. In addition, taking the census approach does not mean that error will not be introduced into your data by nonresponse bias, especially if the people who do not respond differ in some significant way (from the standpoint of your study objectives) from people who do respond.

With a sample, members of the population are selected in some organized way for participation in the survey. Samples are less precise than censuses. The goal in the selection of a sample is to identify a sample that closely matches the population using a random procedure in which each member of the population has an equal chance of being selected. Some type of random or probability sampling is needed if we are to employ inferential statistics, that is, if we are going to be able to use the statistics obtained from the sample to generalize to their corresponding parameters in the population.

When performed properly (e.g., representative sampling, randomization, etc.), sampling can provide extremely reliable estimates of the population and do so in a cost-effective manner. On the other hand, sampling of an already small population (for example, all seniors in a high school) does not gain much in terms of reduced costs and effort. In addition, the margin of error—the likelihood that the data from the response group would not match responses that would be received if a census approach were used—*increases* as the size of a sample respondent group *decreases*. (See the example on the next page.) Thus, with small universes, it simply makes sense to survey everyone.

Estimation of Population Data From
Sample Responses and Determination
of Sample Size

Let's assume that the project objectives identify the need for opinion data from community residents. However, it has been decided that surveying all residents would be too costly. While still in the planning phase, let's use some knowledge about sample statistics to help determine the effect of using two different sample sizes. To do this, we'll need to make an assumption about the percentage of people we think will answer the survey (for the examples below, we'll assume a 30% response rate). We'll also need to decide how close a fit we need between the "picture" the sample responses provides and what we might have gotten if we conducted a census.

Scenario #1

We want to economize. The survey is mailed to only 350 people, about 150 respond. From our past experience with a similar question, we predict—although we certainly don't know for sure—that about 45% of the respondents will respond "no" to a particular question. We can't know that exactly 45% of the people in the population would say "yes." But we can be "90% confident" that the percent of "no" respondents within the population would fall somewhere in the *range* between 37 and 53%.

Scenario #2

Let's increase our sample size to 3,500—with the increase in the size of the sample having a potentially significant effect on the cost of the project. We anticipate responses from about 1,050 people. We could be 90% confident that the percentage of "no" respondents within the population would fall somewhere in the much smaller *range* between 42 and 48%.

Thus, using a larger sample size allows us to predict how the population might respond with a much higher degree of certainty. How important is this in practical terms? Let's consider an example of a bond referendum that we think might be fairly tight, so we want to survey residents about their attitudes before putting the issue on the ballot. While our smaller sample leads us to believe that the referendum would pass, there's still the possibility that the "no" percentage in the universe would actually fall at the high end of the range. Thus, the referendum could fail—we just wouldn't be sure. Using the larger sample allows us to narrow our range of uncertainty and it looks as though the referendum would pass.

Obviously, making estimates such as these involves guesswork—what percentage of people will respond to the survey, will attitudes stay the same between administration of the survey and the actual election, etc. However, keeping the potential impact of sample size in mind when moving on to our next step in the survey process—determining the sample size—can be important.

Notes:_____

_____

_____

_____

_____

_____

_____

_____

_____

_____

_____

_____

_____

_____

_____

_____

_____

_____

_____

_____

_____

_____

_____

_____

_____

_____

_____

Notes:_____

_____

_____

_____

_____

_____

_____

_____

_____

_____

_____

_____

_____

_____

_____

_____

_____

_____

_____

_____

_____

_____

_____

_____

Notes:_____

_____

_____

_____

_____

_____

_____

_____

_____

_____

_____

_____

_____

_____

_____

_____

_____

_____

_____

_____

_____

_____

_____

_____

_____

_____

_____

_____

_____

_____

_____

_____

Chapter 3

Sampling

Step 3. Determine Your Sample Size

There is no simple rule for sample size that can be used for all surveys. Four factors, however, should be considered: the size of the population, the level of precision desired, the level of confidence or risk you are willing to assume, and the degree of variability in the attributes being measured.

Population size. As a general rule of thumb, the larger the sample, the more precisely it reflects the target population. However, the rates of improvement in the precision decreases as the sample size increases. So, it is important to find the right balance between precision and costs of conducting the survey. Oversampling by a large number can increase costs of the survey with perhaps no real gain in the quality of the data collected. Many analysts suggest that about 1,500 persons is a sufficient sample size for most populations. However, consider whether you will want to analyze data from a subgroup of respondents. For a project such as this, there should be at least 50-100 cases within each subgroup. Finally, if your population is small (i.e., under 200 people), it is best to conduct a census rather than sample.

Level of precision desired. The discussion on page 26 provides a concrete example of how sample size can affect sampling error, as indicated by the range around the sample statistic that would likely include the population percentage. This is also known as the confidence interval. It is often expressed in plus or minus percentage points or scores. If a study shows, for example, that 45% of the *sample* supports a change in school boundaries, with a sampling error of plus or minus 5 percentage points, it means that between 40 and 50% of the *population* is estimated to have a similar opinion.

Level of confidence desired. The level of confidence refers to the degree of surety that, if the population were to be repeatedly sampled, the average value of the attribute obtained by those samples would be equal to the true population value. For example, a 95% confidence level means that one can reasonably be confident that 95 out of 100 samples, if drawn, would have the same range around the sample percentage. Typically, 90 and 95% confidence levels are used for sample surveys. Increasing the confidence level requires increasing the number of respondents—and so increasing the size of the sample.

Degree of variability expected in the attributes being measured. The more diverse the population is regarding the attributes being measured, the larger the sample size required. This larger sample size allows us to be more certain that the group of people randomly selected to participate actually represents the population. Likewise, the more similar the population is in terms of the attributes being measured, the smaller the sample size required. The degree of variability can range from .01 to .99, with .50 representing the greatest level of variability. The more one moves away from the .50 midpoint, the less variable the attribute. If you are unsure about the degree of variability, use .50 when determining your sample size because it is the most conservative estimate possible.

A commonsense example can be used to demonstrate. Assume that a community survey is being conducted in a medium-sized town with a very stable and homogenous population. In contrast, a survey could be conducted in a small city that has been experiencing substantial shifts in families moving in and out and is highly diverse in terms of ethnicity and socioeconomic status. Depending on the objectives of the survey project—and so the questions being asked—it might be critical to ensure adequate representation from a variety of subgroups in the second example. Thus, a larger sample size should be used. In the first example, this may not be an issue, and so the sample size could be smaller. Thus, while science can help to some extent with calculating a sample size, there are times when your knowledge of the population is also very important.

Finally, it is important to understand that the statistical approaches developed both for calculating sample sizes and analyzing data address only the issue of representativeness of sample data in general. These techniques do not compensate for the possibility of nonresponse bias. Thus, you could select a sample size that allowed you to be 95% confident of the results, but a low response rate—and even more important, a response rate significantly lower for some subgroups than others—could yield data skewed from the actual opinions of the population.

Methods Used in Determining Sample Size

Sample size formulas take the different factors described above (size of your population, level of precision, confidence level, and degree of variability) into account. However, tables for determination of sample size (see Appendix A) and online "calculators" provide enough information for educators working on home-grown surveys.

Using Tables. The tables provided in Appendix A are both designed around a variability level of .50 (remember, if in doubt, select the highest level of variability, which is

.50). One of the two tables has been calculated using a confidence level of .90, the other uses .95 (you could be more confident of these results than if the .90 table were used). Both of the tables are organized with population size down the side and a range of permissible error across the top (from .05 to .01—this represents sampling error of, for example, + or – 5%), with the intersection between the row and the column indicating the suggested sample size. Let's take a look at an example.

We'll assume that we are conducting a survey of a community with a population of about 5,000 people. Appropriate portions of the two tables are included on the next page so we can review the effects of increasing the confidence level and/or decreasing the level of permissible error.

Let us go first to Table 3.1, which uses a 90% confidence level. The suggested sample size for a population of 5,000 ranges from a low of 257 (permissible error of .05; + or – 5%) to a high of 2,875 (permissible error of .01; + or – 1%). Similar numbers for Table 3.2 (confidence level of 95%) are 357 and 3,288. If you decided that being confident 90% of the time (that a repeated sampling would yield true population values) was a high enough standard, you could use Table 3.1. However, you can also see that raising the confidence level to .95—while still keeping the permissible error at .05—would still allow you to pick a fairly small sample

Table 3.1. Appropriate Sizes of Simple Random Samples

(Variability Level=0.50; Confidence Level=90%)

Population Size	Sample Size for Varying Levels of Permissible Error				
	0.05	0.04	0.03	0.02	0.01
2,000	238	349	546	916	1,544
3,000	248	371	601	1,082	2,078
4,000	253	382	633	1,189	2,514
5,000	257	390	653	1,264	2,875
6,000	259	395	668	1,319	3,180

Table 3.2. Appropriate Sizes of Simple Random Samples

(Variability Level=0.50; Confidence Level=95%)

Population Size	Sample Size for Varying Levels of Permissible Error				
	0.05	0.04	0.03	0.02	0.01
2,000	322	462	696	1,091	1,655
3,000	341	500	787	1,334	2,286
4,000	350	522	842	1,500	2,824
5,000	357	536	879	1,622	3,288
6,000	361	546	906	1,715	3,693

(357 as compared to 257 for the 90% confidence level). Decreasing the level of permissible error within one table increases the size of the recommended sample—on the 90% confidence level table it shifts from 257 to 2,875.

The tables also demonstrate why it typically does not make sense to sample very small populations—for example, the students in a high school enrolling 400 students. If we use the 90% confidence level table and a permissible error of + or -3%, the recommended sample size is 261. This takes us to another important point: *The sample sizes found in tables or through online tools assume a 100% response rate. Thus, you need to adjust the recommended sample size to account for nonresponse* (and you will need to estimate this), which yields a larger actual sample size. Let's use the high school example to demonstrate this.

School enrollment: 400	• Divide (261) by .7 (70% expected to respond)
Anticipated response rate: 70%	• Recommended sample size adjusted for nonresponse: 373
Suggested sample size: 261	

Obviously, it makes sense to survey all students in the school from two perspectives. First, the additional cost will be minimal. Second, there will be no need to estimate universal data from sample statistics. Nonresponse bias aside, the responses received will accurately represent the population.

Two Tips on Sample Size Calculations

Many experts in the field will tell you that 1,000-1,500 participants is generally enough for most surveys. You will need more, however, if your sample will be categorized into subgroups. If you have reason to believe that significant subgroups within the population will differ substantially on key characteristics or opinions, you will need to find a way to sample these subgroups individually or "oversample" the population as a whole (increase the sample size) to ensure you pick up enough respondents from each of the subgroups to permit meaningful analysis of data.

Take expected nonresponse rates into account in your calculation of sample size. To do this, divide the sample size needed by the anticipated *response* rate. For example, if you want no fewer than 500 completed surveys and past experiences lead you to anticipate a response rate of about 30%, you will need to send out 1,667 surveys (500/0.3).

Sample Size Calculators. Another method you can use to determine an appropriate sample size for your study is a sample size calculator. There are several calculators available online. For example, the Creative Research Systems Web site includes an easy-to-use sample size calculator for the 95% level of confidence (online: http://www.surveysystem.com/sscalc.htm). It assumes a .50 level of variability. You plug in information about the level of precision (i.e., confidence interval) desired and the population size, and it will calculate the desired sample size for you.

Step 4. Select a Sampling Method

Proper sampling helps to ensure that the findings generated from your survey reflect the population from which the sample was drawn. There are several methods that you can use to select a sample. These methods generally can be classified into two basic categories: probability and nonprobability sampling.

Probability Sampling. A probability sampling method is any method of sampling that utilizes some form of random selection. There are four commonly used methods of probability sampling:

> *Simple Random Sampling.* With simple random sampling, each member of the population has an equal chance of being selected for participation in your study. For example, say you are interested in sampling community residents about their views on the quality of public education. First, you obtain a list of household addresses in the

community. Next, you mix the addresses so that they are in random order. Then, you randomly select the number of households that you need for your sample.

Using this method, the results obtained can be generalized to the larger population (i.e., the community from which your sample was drawn). However, this method is not always statistically efficient. Specifically, you may get poor representation from subgroups in the population—especially when some subgroups represent only a small portion of the population and may not have adequate representation in your sample.

Systematic Random Sampling. With systematic random sampling, the list is again first put in random order. However, a random starting point is chosen, and every k^{th} member of the population is selected for the sample. Although this method is more precise than simple random sampling, it still has the problem of possibly not producing a sample that is representative of the population.

Stratified Random Sampling. Stratified random sampling (also called proportional or quota sampling) attempts to address the potential problem of underrepresentation of subgroups. The population is first divided into nonoverlapping subgroups (called strata), then a sample is randomly selected from each stratum.

For example, assume that you are interested in community views about the quality of public education (as in the previous example). However, this time you want to examine differences among households with school-age children versus those without school-age children. In this case, you would split your population into two groups based on that criterion. Then, in each group, you would mix the households so that they are in no apparent order. Next, randomly select households from each subgroup.

Stratified random samples will generally yield greater statistical precision than simple random samples or systematic random samples. The additional benefit of stratified random sampling is that it ensures that you will be able to represent not only the overall population, but also key subgroups within the population—especially small subgroups. You can even use different sampling ratios for each subgroup (e.g., oversampling in order to compensate for a small subgroup). When the same sampling ratio is used in each strata, it is known as *proportionate stratified random sampling*.

Likewise, when a different sampling ratio is used in each strata, it is known as *disproportionate stratified random sampling.*

Cluster Sampling. With cluster sampling, the population is first divided into subgroups or clusters. Next, the clusters are randomly selected for inclusion in the sample. Finally, all of the members within the selected clusters are included in the sample. Cluster sampling is used mainly when the population is spread out geographically, and the researcher cannot sample from all of the locations.

Combinations of Sampling Methods. Although we have listed four of the most commonly used sampling methods separately in this section, it is not uncommon for several sampling methods to be used in a single study. For example, cluster sampling could be used in conjunction with simple random sampling, or stratified random sampling could be used in conjunction with systematic random sampling, and so forth. There is no end to the level of complexity that sampling designs may take.

As an example, the National Center for Education Statistics of the U.S. Department of Education uses a combination of sampling methods in its

National Assessment of Educational Progress (NAEP) survey. Samples of schools and students are selected to represent each participating state (stratified random sampling). In an average state, 2,500 students in approximately 100 schools are selected per grade, per subject assessed (cluster sampling and stratified random sampling). The selection of schools is random, within classes of schools with similar characteristics. But some schools or groups of schools (districts) can be selected for each assessment cycle if they are unique in the state. For instance, a particular district may be in the only major metropolitan area of a state or have the majority of a minority population in the state.

As you can see, sampling designs can range from using a single sampling method to using numerous methods in various stages for different groups of members. Keep in mind, however, that adding complexity to your sampling designs will lead to the need for more complex analyses. One of your goals should be to use the simplest, most direct method possible to achieve your objectives.

There may be occasions when a probability sample is not possible for you. In such cases, you may need to sample using a nonprobability sampling approach.

Nonprobability Sampling. Nonprobability sampling is a sampling method in which members of the population are intentionally—not randomly—selected for inclusion in a study. This does not necessarily mean that nonprobability samples are not representative of the population. It does mean, however, that nonprobability samples, technically, do not support inferences about the population.

Why use a probability sample? In general, researchers prefer probabilistic or random sampling methods over nonprobabilistic ones, and consider them to be more accurate and rigorous since everyone in the population has an equal—or almost equal—opportunity to be selected. However, there may be circumstances when it is not feasible or practical to do random sampling. For example, in a school setting, parents who attend a PTA meeting may be asked to respond to a brief survey about parent satisfaction with the report card currently used. Although it is possible that these parents might have different opinions than parents in general, the data collected might be helpful when beginning a discussion about report cards.

There are various kinds of nonprobability sampling methods, but the two most common types are convenience sampling and purposive sampling. With convenience sampling, participants are selected primarily as a matter of handiness or expediency. For instance, research conducted at universities often uses college students in their samples because they are readily available in such . ·a setting. With purposive sampling, on the other hand, members of a population are selected on the basis of the person's meeting specific criteria. For example, medical research studies often recruit volunteers with certain medical conditions. Because the recruitment is voluntary, focused only on those meeting specific criteria, and gathered in a nonrandomized fashion, it is considered a purposive nonprobability sample.

Although nonprobalistic samples are generally considered less desirable than probabilistic samples, they, nonetheless, can provide some indications of opinions or characteristics of the people the nonrandom sample is intended to represent. In some cases, this might be enough to serve your purpose.

Notes:_____

_____

_____

_____

_____

_____

_____

_____

_____

_____

_____

_____

_____

_____

_____

_____

_____

_____

_____

_____

_____

_____

_____

_____

_____

_____

_____

Notes:_____

_____

_____

_____

_____

_____

_____

_____

_____

_____

_____

_____

_____

_____

_____

_____

_____

_____

_____

_____

_____

_____

_____

_____

_____

_____

_____

_____

Notes:_____

_____

_____

_____

_____

_____

_____

_____

_____

_____

_____

_____

_____

_____

_____

_____

_____

_____

_____

_____

_____

_____

_____

_____

_____

_____

Chapter 4

Managing the Survey Process

Step 5. Select a Method of Delivery for Your Survey

A critical decision that you will have to make regarding your survey is how it should be delivered to recipients. There are several options for administering surveys or collecting information from people in other ways. Each has its strengths and weaknesses (see Table 4.1). Below are some questions to ask when considering alternative approaches.

- *Cost.* What is the cost per completed survey? This may be a critical question, particularly if your survey budget is limited. For example, telephone interviews are likely to be more expensive than other approaches if you hire an outside firm to conduct the interviews.

- *Implementation Time.* How long will it take you to get your data? Is it intended to help address a time-sensitive issue for which there is a deadline?

- *Availability of the Sample.* Is a "list" that includes members of the universe about which you want information available—and at a reasonable cost?

- *Is the sample available?* If you are considering a telephone survey, for example, would prospective participants be available to you during work hours, or will you need to contact them at other times of the day?

- *Response Rates.* How high a response rate will you need? For example, if your survey is intended to present only a general indication of community members' desire for new high school programs, a high response rate may not be critical. However, if the survey focuses on voters' intentions in an upcoming bond referendum—and the last referendum was extremely tight—a high response rate could provide you with data that are more likely to be on target and more helpful in planning public relations efforts.

- *Technology.* Can technology—in particular use of a web-based approach—help keep down costs and the time needed for responses? Will use of technology limit the ability of some people to respond?

- *Survey Length.* Do you have a lot of questions to ask? Respondents generally tolerate longer mail surveys and in-person interviews than telephone or computer-based surveys.

• *Sensitivity of the Questions.* Are there sensitive questions in your survey? If so, guaranteed anonymity is especially important.

More About Response Rates

A primary desire of any researcher—and you are certainly a researcher when you are conducting a survey—is to get as high a response rate as he or she can. As was mentioned previously, a low response rate, especially if significant subgroups are underrepresented, can introduce error into your analyses. In addition, the public's perception of the credibility of the data is determined to some extent by the percentage of people who responded.

The type of survey one decides to use may influence the response rate. Mail surveys, for example, tend to have the lowest response rates (typically 10-40%) because of the passive nature in which they are administered. Telephone surveys and in-person interviews, on the other hand, tend to have higher response rates because the researcher has direct interaction with the respondent. With regard to content, market surveys commonly yield 10-15% response rates, while surveys on socially relevant issues about which many of the people surveyed have strong opinions yield about 30-35% response rates.

In addition to the type of survey, a variety of other factors have been identified as affecting response rates. Common reasons for a low response rate include the following:

- Subject matter addressed in the survey is of low interest to the people contacted.

- Survey is too long or not user-friendly.

- There is no direct encouragement or incentive to respond.

Given that surveys are largely voluntary in nature, it is important to do all that you can to encourage participation in your survey. Below are some general tips and considerations for improving your response rate:

- Personalize—include the recipient's name in your cover letter or introduction. This small touch can make a big difference.

- Whenever possible, the cover letter or other communication requesting participation in the study should come from a "recognizable" school or district leader.

- Emphasize that the data collected will be reported only as group statistics, with no response tied to a name.

- Keep the survey short. Ask only the questions for which you need answers. Don't include items if they are not critical to addressing project objectives.

- Make a written survey or one conducted on the web attractive and easy to read. Pay careful attention to the layout of the items, the fonts used, etc.

- Break long surveys into sections.

- Make surveys easy to return by providing postage-paid, preaddressed return envelopes, fax-back capabilities, emailed questionnaires with auto-programmed return, etc.

- Try to include enough time in your schedule for follow-up postcards, emails, or telephone calls to nonrespondents if your response rate is low (usually 2 weeks after the initial administration of the survey).

- Use an up-to-date contact list.

- Include an incentive—describe how the responses will be used, explain how important the respondent's reply is to the survey, provide a summary of findings, etc.

- Oversample to accommodate for nonresponse. However, understand that results from a small sample with a high response rate may yield better data than a large sample with a low response rate.

Survey Delivery Methods

Although the idea that typically comes to mind when the word survey is used is a paper and pencil form, it makes sense to broaden the concept at this point to a variety of ways to collect opinions. Discussions of technical issues, such as random sampling, will not be relevant to all of them. However, there are other technical issues that are relevant to each of them. We'll briefly review four approaches here—personal interviews, group interviews, telephone interviews, and mailed surveys—with the approaches varying in terms of cost, research design, and level of expertise required.

Personal Interviews. Personal interviews are costly and time-consuming for several reasons. The major problems are associated with obtaining an unbiased sample of interviews that truly represent the population studied. Another problem is obtaining a cadre of persons both willing and trained to conduct the interviews. For these and related reasons, personal interview studies are rarely used by school districts to study large populations or groups.

Thus this book will do little more than identify personal interviews as a technique available for use in some types of needs assessment and related surveys.

Group Interviews or Focus Groups. Group interviews or focus groups are also a type of interview and usually can be carried out less expensively than individual interviews. A potentially serious problem with group interviews relates to a lack of representativeness of the group members—especially if a volunteer or open forum approach is used—as related to the universe identified in the objectives. Although the representativeness of the group interviewed to the population studied can create major problems, group interviews can be helpful in developing items to be included in a mail or telephone survey.

Group interviews or focus groups usually involve eight to ten participants in an informal setting, conducted by a trained moderator. The moderator uses an interview schedule but allows the group as much spontaneity as possible within the context of the interview schedule. Questions may be very general in nature, with the intent being to stimulate discussion. Some possibilities for discussion items are presented on the next page.

- What do you *like* most about Northwest Public Schools?

- What do you *dislike* most about Northwest Public Schools?

- Do you have any recommendations for increasing citizen involvement in the schools?

- Are there gaps which need to be closed in our K-12 curriculum? In other words, are there places where we are not preparing students adequately to face society's demands?

- If the school board could make a single addition, change, or improvement in the schools, what would you suggest it should do?

- If you were asked to list the major problems existing in our schools, what would they be?

Using Focus Groups to Gather Information

While the small size of focus groups will typically mean that information generated cannot be considered representative of a much larger population, they can be used to identify questions that should be asked in a mail survey. They can also be used as a follow-up to a mail survey. For example, if only 30% of the respondents to a mail survey felt that the district was doing an acceptable job of teaching basic skills, the focus group could be used to discuss reasons why people felt that way.

The most productive focus groups are not "chat sessions." Instead, they have very specific objectives, established in advance, and these objectives provide clear direction for topics that will be introduced. However, the structure of the sessions should not be so rigid that it limits group interaction, since this is often an important advantage of using focus groups.

Although planning for a focus group is typically less complex than planning for a survey, attention to details will result in better information. Here are some of the tasks that should be addressed before the focus group is held:

- Develop the objective for the focus group. This may include both the topics that will be discussed and a decision about how the information will be used.
- Decide whom to include as participants and invite them. Depending on the purpose of the focus group, it may be helpful to provide them with information in advance.
- Select a moderator/facilitator and, if the session is not being taped, a record-keeper. Provide training as necessary.
- Develop an interview schedule that the moderator will use to guide discussion.
- Develop an instrument to help analyze the data.
- Analyze the data and develop a report.

Skilled moderators are important both for ensuring that the discussion continues to be relevant to the purpose of the session and to help the group reach closure. If more than one moderator is needed, it may be helpful to develop a moderator's guide. This will help both to build consistency into tasks provided to the different groups and to establish the framework for the data analysis necessary at the completion of the focus group activities.

Use of scales or rating systems that the individual members of the group complete at the beginning of the session may be another technique helpful to focusing discussion. Participants are thus able to briefly express their opinions, with the rating scale used again at the end of the session as a means to summarize results.

An important and often-overlooked aspect of collecting data through this method is the significance of demographic information. Information about participants' neighborhoods, whether the participant has children in school, or perhaps even opinions on basic issues should be given consideration when analyzing the recommendations. If the groups are composed predominantly of persons with strong opinions on the topic being discussed—people whose opinions are not representative of those held in the community at large—the usefulness of the data is greatly limited.

Careful consideration should also be given to the scheduling of the sessions. The locations and times at which they are held should make them easily accessible. Sessions held during the school day would, for example, limit attendance by most working people.

An example of the focus group technique was used by one small town school district. The dialogue and needs assessment sessions included 65 randomly selected parents, graduates, senior citizens, students, and members of the faculty, and consisted of: 1) a meeting at which background material and a preliminary questionnaire were distributed and 2) a work session held on a Saturday.

At that time, the attendees were assigned to work in groups of six to eight with a trained moderator to focus on preschool, K-6, and 7-12 educational programs. Each group was provided with dialogue questions and a questionnaire and asked to develop recommendations on a variety of topics.

Another school district held a series of meetings on three Saturdays that included parents, staff, and community members to identify needs and develop goals for the schools. Participants were asked to form eight-person, self-selected groups and discuss the following question: What does our school district need to be doing for its students?

During a 30-minute work session, the groups developed brief statements of needs and recommendations. At the end of the period, groups exchanged statements, discussed and rated each other's comments, and made recommendations about the goals. Groups eventually had their original recommendations returned to them—replete with comments—for review, modification, and prioritizing.

When relevant constituencies are involved, these types of group analysis and input sessions can be useful in identifying problems and generating ideas about possible solutions. In one sense, goals developed through variations of group interview techniques are another way of identifying and stating needs that should be addressed.

Telephone Interviews. Telephone interviews are less costly than individual interviews and can employ random sampling. However, the approach has two major drawbacks. First, an increasing number of people rely on cell phones, which makes getting a useful directory of names and phone numbers difficult. Second, the hectic pace of many people's work days and family responsibilities make them unwilling to be interviewed during the evening.

Other considerations that must be made when considering and planning a telephone survey include cost (if paid rather than volunteer callers are to be used), time of day when calls are to be made, and careful attention to development of the items included on the interview schedule so that they will be understood without the need for repetition or additional explanation. In addition, a form for the recording of responses must be developed. It is important that this form lend itself to efficient data processing.

An aspect of telephone interviewing that cannot be overstated is interviewer training and supervision. Considerable expertise is required on the part of the interviewer, and volunteers should not be used as interviewers unless they have been properly trained. This should include practice in the use of a script, including specific approaches to asking interview questions and recording answers. The interviewer should be familiar with the questionnaire, read the text of the script exactly, and offer no opinions or additional information other than that outlined in the instructions developed.

Also important is the method used by interviewers to introduce themselves and the project. Introduction should be concise and should stimulate interest on the part of the respondents.

Another aspect of quality control is supervision during the time that calling and coding of completed surveys is being accomplished. If done properly, areas of the instrument that are creating problems, as well as interviewers who are deviating from the interview schedule, can be identified promptly, with some opportunity available for improvement.

Sample Introduction to a Telephone Interview

Hello, this is _____ and I'm calling from the Athens School District. We are conducting a survey of parents in the district. The Board of Education wants to know how you would evaluate the current programs and what kinds of program changes you would like. The results of this survey will be used in planning, so it is important for us to talk to you.

All of your answers will be treated in confidence, and no one will be able to identify your individual answers. The interview will take about 15 minutes. Are there any questions you would like to ask before we begin?

A potential problem when using the phone interview approach is the lack of anonymity that comes with interviewing people directly. Persons being called may feel hampered by the feeling that their responses are not anonymous in the same sense that a mail survey can be anonymous. On the plus side, this loss of anonymity may lead to an increased tendency to participate.

From the standpoint of efforts to increase participation by those being called, some school districts mail a letter to members of the sample the week before the calls are made. In addition to stressing the importance of cooperation, the letter can be used to briefly introduce the issues.

Mailed Surveys. Mailed surveys are typically the most economical and should always be based upon random samples of populations or groups to be studied. Nonresponse is a critical problem in mailed surveys. Thus, it is extremely important to use all means possible to achieve a high rate of response.

It is also important to understand that systematic bias in the survey design can lead to some invalid conclusions. For example, mailing survey instruments written solely in English to neighborhoods where many families speak only Spanish may markedly influence the results due to nonresponse by specific groups of people.

While mailed surveys may be the least expensive way to contact large numbers of people, there are also some negative aspects that must be considered. First, the lack of personal contact with the members of the sample makes attention to details that could raise the response rate particularly important. Secondly, the survey instrument must stand on its own without the opportunity for respondents to ask questions, making attention to detail, clarity, and nuance when developing the questions a necessity. Third, questions can be answered out of sequence even if the researcher had a particular order in mind when developing the final draft of the instrument.

On the other hand, the respondent does have the opportunity to look up information which may be requested and anonymity is a more realistic option. If the mailed survey approach is taken, then the number one problem becomes how to achieve a reasonable rate of response. Three factors are important: personalization, persistence, and a well-designed questionnaire. While design of the questionnaire will be discussed in another section, a suggested method for conducting a mailed survey is included here.

After selecting the sample for the survey, a letter outlining the purposes of the survey and the importance of participation should be sent to each person along with the questionnaire and a self-addressed stamped envelope or

business reply envelope. Some important points to consider for inclusion in the survey are listed below:

- Make the communication as personal as possible.

- Outline the purpose of the survey and stress its importance.

- Explain the nature of sample surveys and how the particular sample was selected, stressing that the respondent's answers actually represent many others in the community (or teaching staff, etc.).

- Give the respondent some idea of the time it will take to complete the survey (a short time, only 10 minutes, etc.) and be honest about it.

- Establish a deadline for survey returns.

- Clarify whether or not the responses will be anonymous; even if respondents are asked to provide names for the purpose of follow-up, an explanation that the data will be reported only as numeric summaries may make some potential respondents more comfortable.

- Express appreciation in advance for completion of the survey.

Step 6. Establish a Budget and Timeline for Your Survey

Can you afford a sample size large enough to attain useful results? Do you have the staff time necessary to analyze the date and develop a report? Is there enough "calendar time" available to have data collected before it is needed?

Obviously, the cost of the projected project—along with resources available to support it—are critical elements to consider. It is for this reason that the list of possible budget items (Appendix D) focuses on costs and resources.

A limited budget places constraints on the project in terms of such factors as length of the survey, size of the sample, and method of survey delivery. It simply makes sense to take such constraints into account when planning. For example, you may need to keep the survey short to reduce printing and/or data entry costs. When you begin to estimate costs, be sure to include factors such as staff time in addition to out-of-pocket expenditures.

Table 4.1. Advantages and Disadvantages of Survey Delivery Methods		
	Advantages	**Drawbacks**
Self-Administered Surveys		
Mail Surveys	• Generally they are the least expensive method. • They are the most common method of survey delivery. • They allow respondents to answer at their leisure. • Generally, administration is standardized.	• Time—mail surveys take longer to administer in terms of calendar time than other approaches. • You may need to wait several weeks after the initial mailing to be sure you have gotten all of the responses. • Response rates tend to be lower (typically under 33%). Follow-up requests may be necessary.
Fax Surveys	• Delivery is quicker. • Respondents may answer at their leisure. • Generally administration is standardized. • Response time is generally shorter than mail surveys.	• You will need to have the fax numbers of everyone in your sample. • Not everyone in your sample is likely to have a fax machine. • Technology—if you do not have broadcast fax capabilities, depending on the size of your sample, you may need to contract for this service from an outside source (may be costly).
Email/Web-Based Surveys	• Virtual elimination of data entry and editing costs. • Delivery is quicker. • The novelty can stimulate higher response rates. • Pictures and sound files can be attached. • Speed—the results can be available minutes after completing the survey. • On average, people give longer answers to open-ended questions via the web than they do on other kinds of self-administered surveys.	• The respondents must have access to a computer. • For email surveys, you will need to know the person's email address, which must be up-to-date. • Can lead to selection bias because some people do not have access to computers or email or may not use them regularly. • You may not be able to generalize findings to the whole population. • Without proper security, there may be no control over multiple responses. • Emailing surveys may affect proper formatting. • Some spam systems block email including URLs. • Currently unknown how these methods may affect responses. Research is progressing on the topic.
Interviewer-Administered Surveys		
Telephone Surveys	• Sample can be contacted faster than with the other methods. • If using CATI (computer-assisted telephone interviewing), the system can ensure that questions are skipped when they should be. • Results available quickly if interviewers are entering data during the interview.	• The person must be present to answer the call. • This method can be intrusive and inconvenient unless you notify the person ahead of time that you will be calling. • The dynamics between the interviewer and interviewee may affect responses. • Use of Caller ID systems may affect the number of calls answered.
In-Person Interviews/ Focus Groups	• Direct contact with the person/group of people (more personal). • Can also observe nonverbal responses and dynamics. • Longer surveys are typically tolerated better than paper/pencil or phone surveys. • If the response is unclear or incomplete, the interviewer can follow up. • Surveys tend to be more complete because the interviewer can ensure that all questions are answered.	• Usually more costly per response than other methods • The dynamics between the interviewer and interviewee(s) may affect responses. • Potential for interviewer bias.

Should You Use an Online System? Here Are Some Things to Consider . . .

The use of web-based systems to administer surveys is rapidly growing in popularity. They can be relatively easy to use and some of them are low- to no-cost. However, keep the following questions in mind when deciding whether to use an online system or which one to use:

- Will the online nature of the survey limit some respondents' ability to respond, either through limited access to the web or through inexperience with technology?
- Can the system ensure that only people included in the sample have access to the instrument—and that each of them can answer only once?
- Will respondents find the system easy to use? Does it include features that will make it attractive to users? For example, could a respondent visit the survey once to read it and begin answering items, then return to complete it?
- Do you have confidence in the site and the company hosting it?
- Will the data be secure?
- Have you reviewed the types of questions you will be able to ask and does that capacity address all your needs?
- Does the site have data analysis tools embedded in it? For example, can you automatically generate tables and graphs? In addition, will you be able to download data to your own system for use later or to do more detailed analysis?
- Is there a tool available that generates PDF or HTML files of data highlights? This is a nice, although not essential, feature.

In addition, focus on developing a timeline during the initial planning processes. Knowing how much time you have for each stage of the survey process keeps the survey project focused and on schedule. A helpful approach may be to work backwards from the date when the final report is needed or desired. Moving backwards on a timeline—incorporating all of the tasks that need to be done—provides a more realistic perspective on the project as a whole. Use the timeline during the project to gauge whether it is on track.

For example, if you are using a mailed survey approach, periodically check on the response rate. The week before the information is needed is too late to find out that the response rate is so low that the data will not be considered credible. Instead, set up checkpoint dates and, if the response rate is lower than you'd like, consider sending a follow-up.

Finally, balance these factors with the need for quality. If the "ideal" project looks impossible within the framework of funds, staffing, and/or time available, consider revisiting the objectives. It is often better to address a more narrow set of objectives well than to do a less-than-quality job on a larger set of project goals.

Top Ten Things People Hate About Questionnaires

According to a recent survey conducted by Systems-Thinking.com, an Australian survey research company, the top 10 things people hate about surveys are:

1. too many questions
2. too many free text questions
3. content not appropriate to them
4. poor survey layout
5. lack of anonymity
6. fear of a hidden agenda
7. no logical order to the questions being asked
8. mismatch between question type and response
9. asking about more than one issue per question
10. big gaps between response choices

Notes:_____

_____

_____

_____

_____

_____

_____

_____

_____

_____

_____

_____

_____

_____

_____

_____

_____

_____

_____

_____

_____

_____

_____

_____

_____

_____

_____

Notes:_____

_____

_____

_____

_____

_____

_____

_____

_____

_____

_____

_____

_____

_____

_____

_____

_____

_____

_____

_____

_____

_____

_____

_____

_____

_____

_____

_____

_____

_____

_____

Chapter 5

Creating the Survey Instrument

gain, we point to the critical importance of clearly defined project objectives. They provide both direction and boundaries, in particular placing limits on questions that don't need to be included in the survey development phase.

In addition, the *process* used to identify questions for your survey can add to the value of the data it generates. At some point, one person or a small group of people will be responsible for producing the final draft of the instrument. However, a larger group, including representatives from the groups to be surveyed and those who will be affected by decisions using the survey data, can help to churn ideas about areas of concern and questions. Failure to include these people in the process of survey development may mean that valuable ideas are not considered. Moreover, their participation at this stage may provide a broader base of support later for the decisions made using the survey data.

Step 7. Before You Start Writing

Before you begin developing items for your survey instrument, keep in mind this overarching, golden rule of survey development: Do not start from scratch unless absolutely necessary! Here are some helpful ideas for getting a jumpstart in developing your survey.

Collect Survey Examples

Become a survey junkie. Collect copies of surveys you are sent. Ask your coworkers to forward copies of surveys that they receive to you. It doesn't matter whether the surveys address content similar to the one you are planning. Simply reviewing a variety of surveys is likely to provide you with a broader perspective on what works—and what doesn't. For instance, they can provide ideas about:

- How to word your instructions so that they are clear and easy to understand.

- How your survey should be formatted so that it is attractive and easy to read.

- The ways in which, for example, rating scales should be designed for comprehensiveness and balance.

- Survey items that don't work well and why.

In addition, there may be particular questions on the surveys that are exactly (or similar to) what you want in your survey. Although it is not acceptable to simply reproduce someone else's survey, you can borrow and modify a few of the items to suit the needs of your survey without violating copyright laws.

Obviously, saving examples of surveys is something that you need to do *before* you realize that you need to develop a survey of your own. Start doing this as soon as possible.

Search for Surveys Over the Internet

In addition to collecting surveys that are sent to you, go to a search engine, such as Google or Yahoo, and enter in key phrases such as "parent satisfaction survey." Then scan the results to see if they are what you are looking for. Modify your search accordingly.

Remember that you can always modify your search to be more specific or broad. However, it is best to start off broadly so that you do not inadvertently exclude surveys that may be relevant. If you find that you are retrieving too many items that are not quite what you are looking for, add additional words to narrow your topic. Search stems of key words when there are likely to be many forms of the word in records that may interest you. For example, if you're looking for teacher professional development surveys, using the singular words "teacher" and "survey" will gather records that have the plural form of the words as well. However, if you enter "teachers" or "surveys" in your search, you may only retrieve records that contain the plural form of the words.

A caution—just because a survey was sent to you or you found it online does not mean that it was well designed. In this guide, we will provide some general tips for survey development that will help guide you in developing your own surveys. In addition, the tips can help you discriminate between well-constructed and poorly-constructed surveys.

Reuse Past Surveys

Another strategy you may want to consider is reusing surveys or portions of surveys that were used previously by your school or district. There are several benefits to this:

- If a similar group of people is being surveyed, you will have trend data for comparison.

- If there were problems with any of the items used before (for example, there might have been feedback that people were confused by a question), you can tweak the item to make it better.

• And, finally, it's easier than starting from scratch!

This brings up another point. When creating a survey, be sure to store it electronically so that it can be easily retrieved and reused. It saves time to be able to copy/paste those items into your new survey, doing minor editing as necessary.

Step 8. Develop the Questions for Your Survey

One of the best pieces of advice that a seasoned survey developer can give someone relatively new to the field is to think about how the data will be analyzed while developing the survey items. That is, begin with the end in mind. Mentally draft paragraphs that would report data from an item. Think about charts and graphs you might use. If you know ahead of time how you expect to analyze and use the data, it can help you craft questions that are likely to yield useful results. In addition, it can help you avoid trying to explain responses from an overly complicated question. Simplicity should be your goal in both survey development and report writing.

For example, considering how you intend to report the results of a survey item can help you determine whether it should be responded to with check boxes, as a free-text item, with the use of a rating scale, with a check-all-that-apply option, or some other method. Starting from the end result (reporting) and working backwards (item development) can not only help you determine whether or not you have developed the item in the best way, but can also help identify items that are not terribly useful in meeting your survey goals.

In *Designing and Conducting Survey Research: A Comprehensive Guide*, Rea and Parker (1997) provide some important advice about surveys and survey item development. They state that no questionnaire can be regarded as ideal for soliciting all the information deemed necessary for a study. Most questionnaires have inherent flaws as well as inherent advantages. So, it is up to researchers to use their experience and professional judgment in constructing questions that maximize the advantages and minimize the potential drawbacks of the survey.

With this advice in mind, the following section provides some general tips on surveys and on questionnaire item development that can guide you in minimizing potential drawbacks while constructing a reliable and meaningful survey instrument.

General Considerations

At the risk of sounding repetitive, keep your objectives constantly in mind. The purpose of the survey is to address project goals. Any question that doesn't help with this should not be asked. A second key point—strive for a balance between cost of the project (money, personnel, and time) and comprehensiveness of the survey. Even items that relate to project objectives may need to be eliminated if the project's benefits do not at least equal the resources needed to support it.

Introduction and Cover Letters

Plan to include a brief introduction about the purposes of the survey either at the beginning of the questionnaire or in a separate cover letter. In it, briefly state the purpose of the survey. Explain to respondents that their participation is critical to the success of the study and explain how the data will be used. Provide them with contact information, should they have questions about the survey. Finally, thank them in advance for their participation.

The Cover Letter or Introduction

To motivate recipients to complete your survey, the introduction or cover letter should be short and include the following:

- the purpose of the survey
- why it is important to hear from the potential respondents and how the results might affect them
- a promise of confidentiality, unless there is a specific need to identify people by name (and that would need to be carefully explained)
- the name of the person to contact for questions about the survey
- the due date for completed surveys to be returned
- a fax, email, and/or mail address to which the completed survey should be returned

Figure 5.1. Sample Survey Cover Letter

[DATE]
[RESPONDENT'S NAME]
[RESPONDENT'S ADDRESS]

Dear [RESPONDENT'S NAME]:

The [GROUP CONDUCTING THE STUDY] is conducting this survey in order to [GOAL OR PURPOSE OF SURVEY]. This survey will help [WHO] to better understand [WHAT].

The potential benefits to you for participating in this study are [DESCRIBE BENEFITS]. The results may be helpful in increasing your understanding of [ISSUE BEING INVESTIGATED].

Please take a few minutes to fill out the enclosed survey [HOW] and return it to [WHERE] as soon as possible, or no later than [WHEN]. To thank you for your time and response, you will receive [INCENTIVE (for example, a summary of the results)].

Because the validity of the results depends on obtaining a high response rate, your participation is crucial to the success of this survey. [NOTE WHAT WILL BE DONE WITH THE RESULTS]. Please be assured that your responses will be held in the strictest confidence. All responses will be reported only in aggregate; no identifying information will be reported.

Please do not hesitate to contact [CONTACT PERSON] at [PHONE] or [EMAIL] if you have any questions.

Thank you in advance for your time and help.

Sincerely,

[NAME]
[TITLE]

In addition to providing survey items that directly elicit information about the objectives that you have decided upon, survey instruments often include items to collect other information useful for data analysis. For example:

Demographic Questions. Demographic items allow you to compare the response group to the population it is intended to represent (assuming that there are some characteristics of the population about which you already have information, such as the percentage with children in school). By making comparisons between the known population characteristics and your findings, you will have a better sense of how representative the survey data are. Demographic items also provide the information needed to analyze differences between groups.

Knowledge Questions. Keep in mind: Perception is reality. Knowledge questions help you to determine if, for example, respondents expressing concern about proposed school boundary shifts actually understand what is proposed.

Common Question Types for Surveys

Researchers commonly use four basic types of questions in surveys: multiple choice, open-ended, rating scales, and agreement scales. Examples of each follow.

Multiple Choice Example:

Do you have school-age children?
❏ Yes—they attend the public schools.
❏ Yes—they do not attend the public schools.
❏ No.

There are several advantages to using multiple-choice questions. They are fast and easy to complete, they are easy to administer and score, and they can be used to compare various groups easily. However, because the response options may not include all possible answers, it's possible that responses some respondents may prefer are missing. For example, the options provided to the question above might frustrate someone who had a child in a public school and another in a private setting.

Open-Ended Examples:

What do you feel the high school's most important focus should be in preparing students for their future?

_____

What is the biggest concern that you face in your job as a principal? _____

Open-ended questions allow for spontaneity of responses and also allow us to understand what the respondent thinks by allowing deeper responses to the topic. However, these types of questions require a great deal of time for transcribing and synthesizing responses, and coding of the results may be unreliable (due to difficulty interpreting them, language translation difficulties, illegible handwriting, etc.). In addition, unless the question hits a "hot spot," people may not want to take the time to respond.

Rating Scales Example:

Overall, how would you rate the professional development opportunities in which you've participated this year?

❏ Excellent
❏ Good
❏ Fair
❏ Poor

Rating scales are easy to administer and score, and also allow for group comparisons. In addition, they give you a good sense of the intensity with which the respondent views the topic.

Agreement Scales Example:

To what extent do you agree or disagree with the following statements?

	Strongly Agree	Agree	Neither Agree nor Disagree	Disagree	Strongly Disagree
1. My department works well together as a team.	❑	❑	❑	❑	❑
2. I feel valued at work.	❑	❑	❑	❑	❑

Similar to rating scales, agreement scales—a type of Likert scale—are easy to administer and store, provide a good sense of the intensity of the respondent's views of a topic, and allow for group comparisons quite easily. However, similar to multiple choice items, the options may not include those that the respondent would have chosen and, as a result, may lead to faulty interpretations.

Some Tried and True Tips for Developing Survey Items

General Tips

- **Follow the KISS method–Keep It Short & Simple.** Respect the prospective respondent's time. Ask only those questions that are essential to the primary objectives of your survey. Leave out questions that do not help meet the objectives, no matter how interesting they may be.

- *Think carefully about the characteristics and knowledge of people who will be sent the survey.* For example, asking community members detailed questions about the high school's academic program—especially people who don't have children in high school—would be inappropriate for two reasons. First, you would be unlikely to collect good data. Second, the questions would be frustrating to many of the potential respondents.

- *Attract interest in your survey by its name.* Some people discard surveys based entirely on its subject matter or title. Consider using titles that will pique the interest of the recipient (but make sure that the name accurately reflects the content of your survey).

- *Start with interesting questions*. You want to get people "hooked" in the hope that once they begin answering, momentum will keep them going.

- *Include information about how the respondent should return the survey when it is completed.* This seems obvious, but has been overlooked by survey developers.

- *Consider providing incentives for participation.* Incentives can be an excellent way to increase the response rate of your survey. However, make sure that the incentive is something that the potential respondent would view as a benefit. Incentives do not have to be extravagant gifts. Sometimes merely providing a summary of the survey results can be a large incentive for those participating in your survey.

Survey Items

- ***Avoid emotionally charged wording.*** For instance, don't say: "There is controversy about the possibility that the arts education program in the elementary schools will be drastically reduced. What is your opinion?" Instead, first ask yourself: Why am I asking for opinions? Will the data collected actually affect the final decision? If so, craft neutral questions to gather data that can be useful in that decision-making process.

- ***Do not combine multiple questions into one item.*** For example, asking the following: "Would you support a bond referendum that would be used to pay for a new football field and technology upgrades in all the schools?" might frustrate people who would support one but not the other. In addition, it provides you with less helpful information. Asking about each possibility separately—and then reviewing the data—helps you make better-informed decisions about both the referendum itself and how to sell it.

- **Avoid leading questions.** Questions should be written in ways that do not imply a specific position. For example, a leading question would be "There has been concern expressed that we are losing some of our best teachers since our salaries are not seen as competitive. In your opinion, should teachers get a substantial increase in salary next year?"

- **Avoid questions with long time spans for recall or that require people to "look up" information.** A goal in survey development is to include questions people can answer quickly and accurately without a great deal of effort.

- **Avoid technical terms, acronyms, and jargon unless you are absolutely sure that respondents know what they mean.** For example, do not ask parents "What's your view of the NCLB legislation?" Some parents do not know what NCLB stands for. Similarly, don't ask for opinions about issues with which the potential respondents are not likely to be familiar.

- **Avoid "fill-in-the-blank" questions when you expect a specific range of answers.** Fill-in-the-blank questions are difficult to analyze, and may be difficult to respond to. If you expect certain types of answers, it is best to provide general categories for people to choose from. However, when you want people to brainstorm ideas without limiting their choices, fill-in-the-blank questions are appropriate. This is especially true when you are in the earliest stages of information discovery.

• *Use simple language.* Respondents have a variety of backgrounds, so use simple and easy-to-understand language. For example, rather than asking "In the last month, how frequently have you gone to work using personal transportation?" Instead say: "About how many times in the past month have you driven to work?"

• *Respect respondents' intelligence.* While you should use simple language, do not insult prospective respondents by using overly simplistic or condescending language. Striking a healthy balance between easy-to-understand language and overly simplified language for the respondents' age group and anticipated level of background knowledge is key.

Formatting Tips

> "Format determines the overall impact of a question-naire. The respondent's attitude toward a questionnaire is often determined by how the form looks, not what it contains...It makes no sense to write clear, concise, clean questions only to have them crowded onto the page or printed in type too small to easily read...A clean, logical format also helps...respondents complete the questionnaire" (Cox, 1996, 13-14).

Experts in survey design highlight the importance of the "look" of the survey instrument. They caution that a crowded and difficult-to-read survey is likely to decrease the rate of response. Below are some general formatting tips to help your survey look as professional, easy-to-use, and attractive as possible:

- *Always consider the layout of your survey instrument.* Try to keep your answer spaces evenly aligned. It makes the form easier to read and data entry easier.

- *Put your questions in a logical order.* The issues raised in one question can influence how people think about subsequent questions. Therefore, when applicable, it is better to ask the general question first, and then follow with specific questions.

- **Provide adequate instructions and, if needed, examples.** Do not take it for granted that your respondents know how to complete your survey. Provide clear and specific instructions or examples that give respondents a concrete guide on how to proceed.

- **Use checkboxes rather than blanks.** This will make it obvious to the respondent where and how to mark their responses.

- **Make sure your questions address all of the possible answers.** Allow a "Don't Know" or "Not Applicable" if these are possible responses. Do not force your respondents into picking an invalid response, or one that is "close enough."

- **Balance rating scales.** When the question requires respondents to use a rating scale, make sure that there is room for (and equal use of) both extremes.

- **Do not make the list of survey item choices too long.** If the list of answer categories is long or unfamiliar, it may be difficult for respondents to evaluate all of them.

- **Typeface and font selections.** Select a font style and size that is easy to read. Garamond or Times New Roman are good typeface choices. Use at least 10 or 12 point fonts. Do not use all capitals for anything other than a heading.

- *Question order.* Ideally, the questions in the beginning of a survey should be easy and pleasant to answer, as they tend to encourage participation. However, it is generally advisable to place demographic questions at the end of the questionnaire, as they will seem less intrusive if they appear after the other questions. Grouping questions together by topic also makes the questionnaire easier to answer. Whenever possible, leave difficult or sensitive questions until near the end of your survey. Any rapport that has been built up will make it more likely people will answer these questions.

- ***Consider how the order of answer choices can affect your results.*** Consider varying your positively and negatively worded items throughout the survey to reduce habitual responding. For example, if you have many Likert-type responses (e.g., highly agree, agree, neither agree or disagree, disagree, highly disagree), reorder some of them in the other direction (e.g., highly disagree, disagree, neither disagree or agree, agree, highly agree). However, don't do this in a haphazard way since this risks people, who may not be reading the survey as carefully as you'd like them to, not realizing that you've changed the approach.

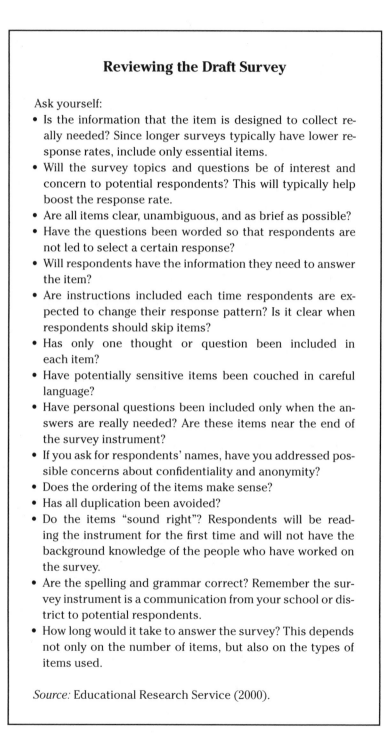

Reviewing the Draft Survey

Ask yourself:

- Is the information that the item is designed to collect really needed? Since longer surveys typically have lower response rates, include only essential items.
- Will the survey topics and questions be of interest and concern to potential respondents? This will typically help boost the response rate.
- Are all items clear, unambiguous, and as brief as possible?
- Have the questions been worded so that respondents are not led to select a certain response?
- Will respondents have the information they need to answer the item?
- Are instructions included each time respondents are expected to change their response pattern? Is it clear when respondents should skip items?
- Has only one thought or question been included in each item?
- Have potentially sensitive items been couched in careful language?
- Have personal questions been included only when the answers are really needed? Are these items near the end of the survey instrument?
- If you ask for respondents' names, have you addressed possible concerns about confidentiality and anonymity?
- Does the ordering of the items make sense?
- Has all duplication been avoided?
- Do the items "sound right"? Respondents will be reading the instrument for the first time and will not have the background knowledge of the people who have worked on the survey.
- Are the spelling and grammar correct? Remember the survey instrument is a communication from your school or district to potential respondents.
- How long would it take to answer the survey? This depends not only on the number of items, but also on the types of items used.

Source: Educational Research Service (2000).

- *Limit open-ended questions.* Open-ended questions are difficult to analyze statistically, although they do provide more detailed qualitative information. Also, prospective respondents typically do not like too many open-ended questions, which can influence your response rate, so try to limit these as much as possible.

- *Provide adequate space.* Experts agree that adequate space for responding should be provided in surveys. They also agree that enough white space should be provided so that the instrument looks easy to complete.

Step 9. Pilot Test Your Survey

Whenever possible, pretest your survey. A pretest enables you to identify potential problems or glitches with a survey item before the survey is conducted. Review the responses from the pretest. In addition, solicit feedback from your pretest sample. Ask them, for example, about their views on the survey's length, clarity, presentation, etc. They also may be able to provide you with response options to questions that you may not have even considered.

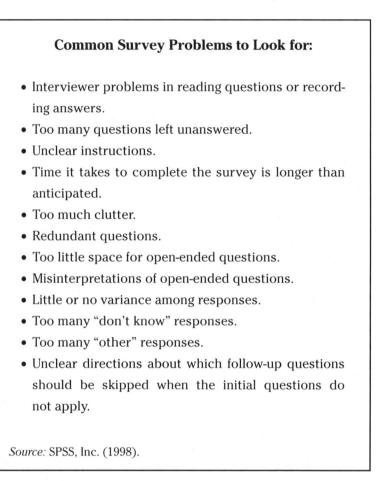

Common Survey Problems to Look for:

- Interviewer problems in reading questions or recording answers.
- Too many questions left unanswered.
- Unclear instructions.
- Time it takes to complete the survey is longer than anticipated.
- Too much clutter.
- Redundant questions.
- Too little space for open-ended questions.
- Misinterpretations of open-ended questions.
- Little or no variance among responses.
- Too many "don't know" responses.
- Too many "other" responses.
- Unclear directions about which follow-up questions should be skipped when the initial questions do not apply.

Source: SPSS, Inc. (1998).

Who should be included in your pretest? For a fresh perspective, having anyone other than the people involved in developing the survey is a good idea.

After pretesting your survey, make the revisions that you found necessary to improve it. Then, give your survey another round of intense examination. If you find that there are any survey items that are not meeting expectations, now is the time to change them.

> "As you think through all the steps in setting up and completing a questionnaire, remember this: You are taking an individual's time and energy, as well as your own time and energy, to put a questionnaire together and to analyze it. Think through all the steps, research the topics, and think about the people involved before you begin. Treat each questionnaire as a scientific instrument, not as just a list of questions to ask people" (Bernhardt, 1998, p. 264).

Notes:_____

_____

_____

_____

_____

_____

_____

_____

_____

_____

_____

_____

_____

_____

_____

_____

_____

_____

_____

_____

_____

_____

_____

_____

_____

_____

_____

_____

Notes:_____

_____

_____

_____

_____

_____

_____

_____

_____

_____

_____

_____

_____

_____

_____

_____

_____

_____

_____

_____

_____

_____

_____

_____

_____

_____

_____

Notes:_____

_____

_____

_____

_____

_____

_____

_____

_____

_____

_____

_____

_____

_____

_____

_____

_____

_____

_____

_____

_____

_____

_____

_____

_____

_____

_____

_____

Chapter 6

Reviewing and Analyzing Your Responses

Step 10. Data Analysis

In this section, we will briefly discuss reviewing survey data and the common types of analyses performed with surveys.

Quality Control of Survey Data

One of the first steps in analyzing survey data is implementing quality control procedures. This may sound complex, but it is not difficult. Quality control actually begins during survey design. By including only well-crafted items in the survey instrument, you reduce the chance that respondents will provide misleading answers. In addition, any data entry procedures should be intentionally designed to guard against error.

However, there are still potential problems you should be ready to address. For example, how will you handle a situation when the respondent marks two of the options of a multiple choice question or agreement scale in which they were told to select only one response? If data are missing for any given item, how are you going to code (i.e., enter) them? Having a clear plan before you begin data entry will help to produce better data. If more than one person is reviewing completed survey forms, be sure they all understand how to treat such situations.

If data from the surveys are entered manually, perhaps into a database or spreadsheet, spot check the accuracy of data entry and also consider building data checks into the data entry process. For example, if respondents were asked to specify a number in a range from one to five, the system should reject any other possibilities. Finally, the program you use to analyze the data can be built to identify discrepancies. For example, if you asked parents to indicate how many children they had in school, a figure of 27 in the database should be kicked out as a problem.

As a general rule, you want to retain as much data as you can, but do not allow highly questionable or erroneous data to be included in your analysis. Doing so may dramatically affect your results and lead to faulty interpretations.

"Without proper checking, errors may go undetected....
Murphy's Law applies here: 'If anything can go wrong
it will.'...

The corollary is even more important: 'If you didn't
check on it, it did.'"

Source: Section on Survey Research Methods (1997).

Once you are confident that your data are accurate and
that the responses are likely to reflect a representative
sample of the population, you can begin to use whatever
software program you have chosen to analyze your data.
(Note: SPSS and SAS are common statistical programs, but
for simple analyses, you can use a spreadsheet program,
such as MS Excel or Lotus).

Commonly used analysis techniques for surveys include:

- Descriptive statistics (e.g., percentages of specific responses and average responses)

- Comparisons (e.g., group differences)

- Trends (e.g., comparison of results over time)

Typically, when reporting survey results, you will want to report them in terms of percentages. A percentage reflects the number of persons responding to your survey in a particular way divided by the total number of persons who should have responded to that survey item, all multiplied by 100. For example, suppose you surveyed 30 teachers on which day they would prefer to hold an upcoming staff meeting: Tuesday, Thursday, or Friday. Five teachers picked Tuesday, 8 teachers picked Thursday, 12 teachers picked Friday, and 5 teachers did not answer the question at all. You can report their responses using percentages in the following manner:

Tuesday: 16.7%   *[based on (5/30)*100=16.66]*
Thursday: 26.7%   *[based on (8/30)*100=26.66]*
Friday: 40.0%   *[based on (12/30)*100=40.00]*
No Response: 16.7%   *[based on (5/30)*100=16.66]*

Note the percentages should sum to 100%, but may be slightly off (generally about 0.1 or 0.2 percentage points) due to rounding. For example, the percentages in the example summed to 100.1%. If you plan to round your percentages, include a footnote explaining that percentages may not sum to exactly 100%, due to rounding.

In the above example, five people did not respond to the survey question. It is common to have people who either do not respond to a survey question or who respond in a way that is unclear. In such cases, the question is generally treated as a nonresponse. You may want to streamline reporting by including percentages only for *valid* responses, since a nonresponse to a survey question occurs frequently. Using only valid responses will increase your percentages slightly, as it is no longer necessary to report the nonresponse percentage of each survey question.

To illustrate, using the above example, if valid responses were used, the results would be:

Tuesday:	20.0%	*[based on (5/25)*100=20.00]*
Thursday:	32.0%	*[based on (8/25)*100=32.00]*
Friday:	48.0%	*[based on (12/25)*100=48.00]*

Note that the denominator changed from 30 to 25 because five teachers did not provide any response to the question. Thus, the total number of valid responses was reduced to 25. This yielded slightly larger percentages for each response. When you report the data for this item, it is helpful to precede the information by the phrase "Of the teachers who selected an option." An alternative would be to include a note in the introduction to your report that states all percentages were calculated using people who responded to the item as a base.

Typically, only valid responses are reported for survey data, however either method is fine. Just remember to include percentages for the nonresponses if you decide not to limit your analysis to valid responses only.

Generating percentages can be done easily using a spreadsheet program, such as Excel, or statistical software, such as SPSS or SAS. Please consult your program instructions for information on obtaining percentages from your data.

Percentages can be provided in terms of overall results and can also be presented for various subgroups surveyed. Additionally, some studies will provide trend data to display changes in percentages over time.

Means, or averages, are also commonly computed for items requesting a numeric response (for example, number of children in school, number of PTA meetings attended during the current school year, etc.). Averages are computed by summing each of the valid responses and dividing by the total number of valid responses. For example, if you had a sample of five people whom you asked to provide their age, with the following responses: 20, 30, 30, left blank, and 25, you compute the average age of the respondents by summing 20+30+30+25, and dividing the total by four. This would yield an average age of 26.3 years. Notice that the sum was divided by four, rather than five, because there were only four *valid* responses to the question.

Since your survey is likely to yield more than five responses, you will want to use a spreadsheet program, such as MS Excel, or statistical software, such as SPSS or SAS, to compute your means. Please consult these software programs specifically for more information on computing means.

Notes:_____

_____

_____

_____

_____

_____

_____

_____

_____

_____

_____

_____

_____

_____

_____

_____

_____

_____

_____

_____

_____

_____

_____

_____

_____

_____

Notes:_____

_____

_____

_____

_____

_____

_____

_____

_____

_____

_____

_____

_____

_____

_____

_____

_____

_____

_____

_____

_____

_____

_____

_____

_____

_____

_____

Notes:_____

_____

_____

_____

_____

_____

_____

_____

_____

_____

_____

_____

_____

_____

_____

_____

_____

_____

_____

_____

_____

_____

_____

_____

_____

_____

Chapter 7

Final Steps: Getting the Word Out

Step 11. Reporting Your Results

Collecting survey data and then failing to report and disseminate the information would be a mistake. Public monies have been spent and some product is expected. Constituencies with a stake in decisions they assumed would be affected by the results of the survey will be waiting for the results. Perhaps worst of all, decisions that could profit from a formal reporting of the data will be made without it. It should be assumed from the outset that an important part of the project will be the preparation of a report and the dissemination of information.

The text of the report should be clear and concise, with efforts made to keep the need for an understanding of statistics to a minimum. When possible, it is helpful to illustrate the comments with charts or graphs. These can often make the point stronger than either a verbal explanation or tables.

One of the simplest ways to report your survey results is to reproduce your survey instrument, then add the percentages for each response to the response options. This provides a relatively quick and easy way to display overall survey results.

Alternatively, you can present your survey results in tables. For example, you can report teachers' responses to the survey question in the previous example as:

1. Which day would you prefer that we hold our upcoming staff meeting?

Day of the Week	Percentage
Tuesday	20.0
Thursday	32.0
Friday	48.0

Sometimes a graphic display—either alone or in combination with a table—provides the best "picture" of the data. The staff meeting example could be graphically displayed in the following manner:

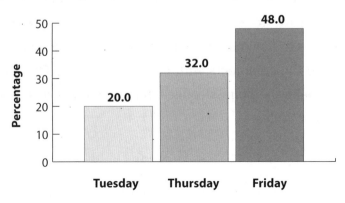

The data could also be displayed as a pie chart in the following manner:

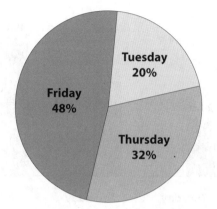

If you wish to provide results for various respondent subgroups, tables, charts, and graphs are far superior to reproducing the survey instrument with obtained percentages. For example, suppose that, rather than asking only teachers about their preference for the upcoming staff meeting, you wanted to know whether various groups of staff had different preferences. If, for example, you wanted to compare responses of teachers with those of other support staff, your results may be displayed in the following manner:

Day of the Week	Percentages	
	Teachers	Support Staff
Tuesday	20.0	34.1
Thursday	32.0	12.2
Friday	48.0	53.7

Alternatively, you could present this data graphically as follows:

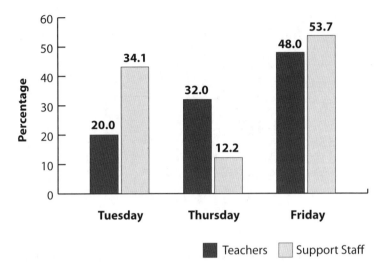

Note that, because there are various subgroups in this example, a pie chart would not be appropriate to use.

A more complex presentation of the results would include text in addition to a table or graph to provide context and highlight key findings. In the example above, the findings could be written in the following manner: "When asked which day they would prefer to hold the upcoming staff meeting, both teachers and support staff preferred Friday as their first option. Friday was the preferred day for 48% of the teachers and 53.7% of the support staff. However, staff differed with regard to the second most preferred day. Slightly over one third of the support staff preferred Tuesday, whereas 32.0% of the teachers preferred Thursday for the staff meeting."

"Excellence in survey practice requires that survey methods be fully disclosed and reported in sufficient detail to permit replication by another researcher and that all data (subject to appropriate safeguards to maintain privacy and confidentiality) be fully documented and made available for independent examination. Good professional practice imposes an obligation upon all survey and public opinion researchers to include, in any report of research results, or to make available when that report is released, certain minimal essential information about how the research was conducted to ensure that consumers of survey results have an adequate basis for judging the reliability and validity of the results reported. Exemplary practice in survey research . . .(a) [describes] how the research was done in sufficient detail that a skilled researcher could repeat the study, and (b) [makes] data available for independent examination and analysis by other responsible parties (with appropriate safeguards for privacy concerns)."

Source: The American Association of Public Opinion Research (n.d.)

This type of more formal report is often needed if, for example, the school board has requested the information to help them review an important issue. Or you might develop a brief report that still included both graphs and text to distribute to parents or the media.

When developing a formal survey report, it is best to provide a concise description of your entire process from start to finish (from your stated objectives to your results and conclusions). Your report should tell the story of your journey and findings in a logical and understandable way, so that the context of the findings are better understood by readers and so that those interested can replicate your study, if desired.

The American Association for Public Opinion Research (2003) suggests some elements that should be included in a formal survey report. Take a minute to review and decide which of these—and in how much detail—should be addressed in your report:

- Who sponsored the survey, and who conducted it.

- Purpose of the study, including specific objectives.

- Survey instrument and/or the exact, full wording of all questions asked, including any visual exhibits, and the text of any preceding instruction or explanation to the interviewer or respondents that might reasonably be expected to affect the response.

- Definition of the universe (i.e., the population under study which the survey is intended to represent) and a description of the sampling frame used to identify this population, including its source and likely bias.

- Description of the sample design, including cluster size, number of callbacks, information on eligibility criteria and screening procedures, method of selecting sample elements, mode of data collection, and other pertinent information.

- Description of the sample selection procedure, giving a clear indication of the methods by which respondents were selected by the researcher (or whether the respondents were entirely self-selected) and sufficient detail of how the sample was drawn to permit fairly exact replication.

- Size of samples and sample implementation, including a full accounting of the final outcome of all sample cases: total number of sample elements contacted, those not assigned or reached, refusals, terminations, noneligibles, and completed interviews or questionnaires.

- Documentation and a full description, if applicable, of any response or completion rates cited (e.g., for quota designs, the number of refusals) and, whenever available, information on how nonrespondents differ from respondents.

- Description of any special scoring, editing, data adjustment or indexing procedures used.

- Discussion of the precision of findings, including, if appropriate, estimates of sampling error with references to other possible sources of error, so that a misleading impression of accuracy or precision is not conveyed, and a description of any weighting or estimating procedures used.

- Description of all percentages on which conclusions are based.

- Clear delineation of which results are based on parts of the sample, rather than on the total sample.

- Method(s), location(s), and dates of interviews, fieldwork or data collection.

- Interviewer characteristics.

- Copies of interviewer instructions or manuals, validation results, codebooks, and other important working papers.

- Any other information that a layperson would need to make a reasonable assessment of the reported findings.

Bernhardt (1998) adds that recommendations and steps for future study should also be included, when applicable and appropriate.

The methodology used also deserves some attention. In addition to including a description of the sampling approach used, this section should clearly identify the limitations of sample surveys in general and, more important, of this particular sample survey.

For example, if nonresponse rate was higher for one of the sample groups than for others—for example, the universe of recent past high school graduates—this fact should be clearly stated. If a less than ideal list was used in sample selection because it was the only one available, that should be explained. Generally, it is better to present a study's limitations honestly, while not overstating them. This will add rather than detract from the legitimacy of the data.

In addition, it's often useful to anticipate ways in which people dissatisfied with the results of the survey might attack it from a technical perspective and respond. For example, see the two examples below:

- "Since the survey shows that 66% of the citizens would support increased taxes to improve education, why not consider a local surtax to increase monies for the schools?" District Response: Although 66% of the people did favor increased taxes for education, they were evenly divided in opinion regarding whether this additional money should come from local, state, or federal taxes. Since only one third of the 66% of the people favoring increased taxes thought local taxes should be raised, this indicates only about 22% of the people in this school district would vote in favor of a local surtax. This figure is very close to the percentage of the voters who cast their ballots in support of a local surtax for the schools in the last election.

- "Why were so few parents (26%) included in the survey?" District Response: The sampling technique used to select interviewees for the survey was designed to reflect the population makeup of this school district. Since less than 30% of the residents have school-age children, the survey provides an accurate sampling of the citizens residing in this school district.

Organizing the report so that readers can easily find exactly what they want to know adds to its usefulness. If your report is more than just a few pages long, you might consider including an abstract or summary as well as a short table of contents. Overarching goals should be to:

- Write clearly and with your audience in mind.

- Present findings in a way that will not lead to misunderstandings or overreaching of the import of the results.

- Have the report available in time to support the need for information around which the project was originally designed.

Step 12. Utilizing the Findings of the Survey

The report has been written—what happens now? If the report writing phase included recommendations for changes or improvements, some of "what should happen now" is already in outline form.

However, it is at this stage of the survey project that the data should be carefully tied back to the project objectives. The data collected may provide not only an identification of the "problem" but a justification for action. Proposed solutions or courses of action will have to be evaluated, decisions made, and actions implemented.

When reviewing the data and related proposals, one question is especially important. Were there some proposed goals implicit in the objectives? If so, these goals should now be reviewed from the perspective of the new information available. As one of the final steps, responsibilities for action must be assigned.

Utilizing Findings From the Survey Project

- restatement of objectives
- review of data
- development and evaluation of solutions
- identification of actions and recommendations to decision makers
- communication of decisions

As was the case with the reporting of the results of the survey, attention should be given to communicating the goals and action developed using the survey data plans. Special attention should be given to communication with affected parties, although the general public should not be overlooked. In addition, it may be appropriate to develop an action plan. Questions that might be addressed in the drafting of an action plan include:

- What will happen now? This question should be addressed both from the standpoint of the final anticipated outcome and from the activities that will be needed to achieve this outcome.

- What might be the effect of these activities on other school and district operations?

- What are the dates at which each of these activities are planned to begin and end?

- Who is responsible for work, monitoring, etc., related to each of these activities?

- What indicators should be used to assess completion, success, etc., of the components of the plan and at what points should these checks be made?

- Who will be informed about the action plan and how will this communication take place?

In addition to moving the school or district agenda forward, the development and communication of the plan further demonstrates that the expenditure of resources on the survey project was worthwhile.

Listen carefully to what the public is saying—and use polling data wisely. Education has discovered publicity polling, along with the value of hard data. The pressure to document results has increased appetites for opinion data that highlight changes in attitudes toward education. Like their counterparts in the corporate arena, education leaders who want to get their issues in the news have come to understand the value of quantifying information to satisfy media and public demand for hard numbers.

But snapshot surveys tell only part of the picture, from one moment in time, and, as such, may not merit or portend changes in policy or practice. Words in opinion polls mean many different things. Consider the danger of "stop thought" words, loaded with connotations that thwart discussion and make many polling questions trivial. And remember, attitudes toward education are influenced by the larger fabric of public opinion, just as schools reflect the larger conditions in society (Widmeyer, 2006).

A Closing Note

Community surveys can be a valuable tool for school and school district leaders. They can provide solid data to guide important decisions regarding school improvement, instructional programs, and district policy. In addition, reaching out to community members and asking for their views communicates to stakeholders that their participation in schools is important and valued.

However, a critical assumption underlies these statements about the potential value of surveys. They must be done well from a technical perspective. They must be cost-effective—both from the perspective of actual cost and benefits and in terms of people's perceptions about the value of the survey data in support of school and district processes. And they must answer the questions they were originally intended to address. Knowledge of some technical how-to's, careful planning, and attention to detail can ensure each of these happens.

One last set of to-do's can help with future survey projects. Review and discussion after the survey is completed is a worthwhile expenditure of time if you address questions like these:

- Could something have been done differently to increase the response rate?

- Did respondents write notes on the surveys that indicated some questions were difficult to answer? Or, did their notes identify areas of concern that might be addressed on another survey?

- Were critical groups left out of the discussion about project objectives?

- Are there ways the survey might have been conducted less expensively?

Discussing issues such as these while they are still fresh in the minds of the people who worked on the project can provide valuable information that can be used to make the next community survey even better.

Finally, it is important that everyone involved in the project keep this thought in mind from the outset: Information collected from surveys does not make policy nor allocate resources. Although survey data can be a valuable addition to the decision making process, knowledge, common sense, and experience on the part of decision makers are also valuable. And it is people who make the decisions.

Best of luck with your survey project!

References and Resources

American Association for Public Opinion Research. (n.d.). *Best practices for survey and public opinion research.* Retrieved from http://www.aapor.org/bestpractices.

Bedrosian, O. T., & Kritch, C. (1990). Building community support through a needs assessment survey. *ERS Spectrum, 8*(3), 35-39.

Bernhardt, V. L. (1998). *Data analysis for comprehensive schoolwide improvement.* Larchmont, NY: Eye on Education.

Bracey, G. W. (2003). *Understanding education statistics: It's easier (and more important) than you think.* Arlington, VA: Educational Research Service.

Covey, S. R. (1990). *The seven habits of highly effective people.* New York: Free Press.

Cox, J. (1996). *Your opinion, please! How to build the best questionnaire in the field of education.* Thousand Oaks, CA: Corwin Press.

Drott, C. M. (n.d.). *Dr. Drott's random sampler: Setting a value for variability.* Retrieved from http://drott.cis.drexel.edu/sample/variability.html

Educational Research Service. (2000). *Conducting community surveys to guide educational decisions and build public support.* The Informed Educator. Arlington, VA: Author.

Ferber, R., Sheatsley, P., Turner, A., & Waksberg, J. (1980). *What is a survey?* Washington, DC: American Statistical Association.

Fink, A., & Kosekoff, J. (1985). *How to conduct surveys: A step-by-step guide.* Newbury Park, CA: Sage Publications.

House, J. I. (1989). The exit poll: An environmental scanning technique for school districts. *Planning and Changing,* 244-254.

InfoPool. (n.d.) *How to write a good survey.* Retrieved from www.accesscable.net/~infopoll/tips.htm.

Israel, G. D. (1992). *Determining sample size.* Retrieved from http://edis.ifas.ufl.edu/BODY_PD006.

National Center of Education Statistics. (2007). *The nation's report card: How the samples of schools and students are selected for the main assessments (state and national).* Retrieved from: http://nces.ed.gov/nationsreportcard/about/nathow.asp.

NEA Research Division. (1965). *Sampling and statistics handbook for surveys in education.* Washington, DC: National Education Association.

Pearson NCS. (2003a). *Research notes: How many people are enough? A lesson in sampling.* Retrieved from http://survey.scantron.com/resources/planning/people.htm.

Pearson NCS. (2003b). *Survey research notes: Data collection methods.* Retrieved from http://survey.scantron.com/resources/implementation/data_collection.htm.

Rea, L. M. & Parker, R. A. (1997). *Designing and conducting survey research* (2nd ed.). San Francisco: Jossey-Bass Publishers.

Roden, J. K. (1998, Fall). 4 ways to make a survey slip and fall. *Journal of Staff Development,* 28-32.

Section on Survey Research. (1997). *How to collect survey data.* Alexandria, VA: American Statistical Association.

SPSS Inc. (1998). *SPSS survey tips.* Chicago, IL: Author. Retrieved from http://www.spss.com/PDFs/STIPlr.pdf.

SystemsThinking.com. (n.d.) *Top ten things people hate about surveys.* Retrieved from http://www.systemsthinking.com.au/tips.html

Thomas, S. J. (1999). *Designing surveys that work! A step-by-step guide.* Thousand Oaks, CA: Corwin Press, Inc.

Wiggins, G., McTigh, J. (1998). *Understanding by design.* Alexandria, VA: Association for Supervision and Curriculum Development.

White, P. (1998). *How much time is needed for a survey?* Retrieved from http://www.cems.uwe.ac.uk/~pwhite/SURVEY3/node18.html.

Widmeyer, S. (2006, June 6). Communicating for change: What educators must know and be able to do [Electronic version]. *Education Week.* Retrieved from http://www.edweek.org/ew/articles/2006/06/07/39widmeyer.h25.html

Appendix A: Determining Sample Sizes

Table A.1. Appropriate Sizes of Simple Random Samples

(Variability Level=0.50; Confidence Level=90%)

Population Size	Sample Size for Varying Levels of Permissible Error				
	0.05	0.04	0.03	0.02	0.01
100	73	81	88	94	99
200	115	136	158	179	194
300	142	175	214	255	287
400	161	206	261	323	378
500	176	229	300	386	466
600	186	248	334	443	551
700	195	264	362	495	634
800	202	277	388	543	715
900	208	288	410	587	794
1,000	213	297	429	628	871
2,000	238	349	546	916	1,544
3,000	248	371	601	1,082	2,078
4,000	253	382	633	1,189	2,514
5,000	257	390	653	1,264	2,875
6,000	259	395	668	1,319	3,180
7,000	261	399	679	1,362	3,440
8,000	262	402	687	1,396	3,665
9,000	263	404	694	1,424	3,862
10,000	263	406	699	1,447	4,035
15,000	266	411	716	1,520	4,662
20,000	267	414	724	1,559	5,055
25,000	268	416	730	1,584	5,324
30,000	268	417	733	1,601	5,520
40,000	269	418	738	1,623	5,786
50,000	269	419	741	1,636	5,959
75,000	270	420	744	1,654	6,205
100,000	270	421	746	1,663	6,336
500,000	270	422	751	1,686	6,675
1,000,000	271	423	751	1,688	6,720
2,000,000	271	423	751	1,690	6,742

Table A.2. Appropriate Sizes of Simple Random Samples

(Variability Level=0.50; Confidence Level=95%)

Population Size	Sample Size for Varying Levels of Permissible Error				
	0.05	0.04	0.03	0.02	0.01
100	79	86	91	96	99
200	132	150	168	185	196
300	168	200	234	267	291
400	196	240	291	343	384
500	217	273	340	414	475
600	234	300	384	480	565
700	248	323	423	542	652
800	260	343	457	600	738
900	269	360	488	655	823
1,000	278	375	516	706	906
2,000	322	462	696	1,091	1,655
3,000	341	500	787	1,334	2,286
4,000	350	522	842	1,500	2,824
5,000	357	536	879	1,622	3,288
6,000	361	546	906	1,715	3,693
7,000	364	553	926	1,788	4,049
8,000	367	558	942	1,847	4,364
9,000	368	563	954	1,895	4,646
10,000	370	566	964	1,936	4,899
15,000	375	577	996	2,070	5,855
20,000	377	583	1,013	2,144	6,488
25,000	378	586	1,023	2,191	6,938
30,000	379	588	1,030	2,223	7,275
40,000	381	591	1,039	2,265	7,745
50,000	381	593	1,045	2,291	8,056
75,000	382	595	1,052	2,327	8,514
100,000	383	597	1,056	2,345	8,762
500,000	384	600	1,065	2,390	9,423
1,000,000	384	600	1,066	2,395	9,513
2,000,000	384	600	1,067	2,398	9,558

*As an alternative, use the online calculator at
http://www.surveysystem.com/sscalc.htm.

Appendix B: Survey Management Worksheet

Survey Mission: _____
_____
_____

Objective 1:
_____
_____
_____

Objective 2:
_____
_____
_____

Objective 3:
_____
_____
_____

Sources of Other Information to Be Used: _____
_____
_____

Prospective Participants: _____

Census / Sample: If sample, sample size: _____

Survey Delivery Method to Be Used:_____

Once Gathered, Data Will Be Used to: _____
_____
_____

Survey Team

Name   Roles
_____   _____
_____   _____
_____   _____
_____   _____

Appendix C: Timeline

Project Start Date: _____

Number and Dates of Survey Follow-ups:_____

_____

Due Date for Completed Survey Results/Report: _____

_____

Tasks and Time Estimates
(These Stages May Overlap)

	Begin Date	Time Needed
Planning Phase:	_____	_____
Survey Instrument Development:	_____	_____
Pilot Testing and Analysis:	_____	_____
Survey Revision:	_____	_____
Data Collection Planning:	_____	_____
Producing and Distributing Surveys:	_____	_____
Receiving Completed Surveys:	_____	_____
Summarizing Data:	_____	_____
Preparing Report:	_____	_____

Estimated Date When Project Can Be Completed: _____

Appendix D: Possible Budget Items

Staff time for planning the study and steering it through the various stages. $_____

Labor and material costs for pretesting the questionnaire and field procedures. $_____

Supervisory costs for interviewer hiring, training, and supervision. $_____

Interviewer labor costs and travel expenses (and meals and lodging, if out-of-town). $_____

Labor and material costs for editing, coding, and entering the information from the questionnaire onto computer.

                                                $_____

Cost of spot-checking to assure the quality of the editing, coding, and data entry. $_____

Cost of cleansing the final data (i.e., checking the data for inconsistent or impossible answers). $_____

Programming costs for preparing tabulations and special analyses of the data. $_____

Labor time and material costs for analysis of the data and report preparation. $_____

Telephone charges, postage, reproduction, and printing costs. $_____

Adapted, with modifications, from Thomas (1999) and White (1998).

Appendix E: Checklists

Checklist: Items to Include in Your Cover Letter or Introduction

❏ Does it include the recipient's name?

❏ Is the letter personally signed (preferably by a high-ranking person)?

❏ Is the purpose of the survey clearly stated?

❏ Does it explain why it is important to hear from the recipient and how he or she will benefit from responding?

❏ Does it include an incentive for responding?

❏ Does it explain what may be done with the results and what possible impacts may occur based on the results?

❏ Does it emphasize confidentiality?

❏ Does it identify a person to contact for questions about the survey?

❏ Does it include a due date for the completed survey, and is it an acceptable amount of time?

❏ Does it include a fax, email, and/or mail address to which completed surveys should be sent?

❏ Does it include a self-addressed, postage-paid envelope (if it is to be returned by mail)?

❏ Is the questionnaire easy to return (e.g., with preaddressed return envelopes, 800 number telephone response, etc.)?

Checklist: Items to Include in Your Report
(if applicable)

❏ Does it include who sponsored the survey, and who conducted it?

❏ Does it include the purpose of the study, including specific objectives?

❏ Does it include the questionnaire and/or the exact, full wording of all questions asked?

❏ Does it include a description of the sampling frame and sample selection procedures?

❏ Does it include information about the sample size, number of refusals, terminations, noneligibles, etc.?

❏ Does it include documentation and a full description of response or completion rates?

❏ Is there a description of any special scoring, editing, data adjustment, or indexing procedures used?

❏ Is there a description of all percentages on which conclusions are based?

❏ Is there clear delineation of which results are based on parts of the sample, rather than on the total sample?

❏ Is there any other information that a layperson would need to make a reasonable assessment of the reported findings?

Other Available Resources

ERS Resources

Understanding Education Statistics: It's Easier (and More Important) Than You Think, Second Edition, by Gerald W. Bracey, 2003. (Stock No. 0496). Base price: $20 (subscriber discounts available).

This guide discusses both descriptive and inferential statistics, including measures of central tendency and dispersion, correlation, *t*-tests, analysis of variance, and when and how to use nonparametric statistics. It also provides useful tips to help you critically evaluate research.

Other Resources

Sample Surveys
Web sites that contain samples of surveys that can be viewed or modified for use:

http://www.sun-associates.com/eval/samples/ samplesurv.html
Sun Associates provides a sample teacher survey that assesses the effectiveness of instructional technology and its implementation across a school district.

http://goal.ncrel.org/winss/winss.htm
Contains eight sample online surveys that help schools assess where they currently are in terms of the seven characteristics of successful schools (vision, leadership, high academic standards, standards of the heart, family-school-community partnerships, professional development, evidence of success).

http://www.teachingquality.org/twc/whereweare.htm
Information on teacher surveys can be accessed through the teacher working conditions portion of the Web site of the Southeast Center for Teaching Quality.

http://www.usaed.net/dev/surtest/stakeholder.html
School Solutions provides a sample of a parent, teacher, and student opinion survey.

http://bdsphd.tripod.com/srv/srv-index.htm
This site contains samples of five surveys:
• *Student Opinion Questionnaire* and *Parent Opinion Questionnaire* (for use in grades 1-8)—assesses student attitudes and opinions or parent perceptions about discipline, classroom climate, school climate, learning environment, staff-student relations, perception of self, and academic success.

- *Opinion Survey for Students* (for use in grades 6-12)—assesses student attitudes and opinions about school climate, discipline/safety, learning environment, staff-student relations, perception of self, and academic progress.
- *Instructional Quality Survey* (for all certificated, classified, and administrative staff)—assesses how well the school stacks up against 13 traits of "effective schools" including program goals and objectives, expectations for students, coordination among programs, parent and community involvement, staff development, leadership, instruction, academic learning time, monitoring student progress, feedback and reinforcement, school and classroom climate, recognizing excellence, and using evaluation results.
- *Open Schools/Healthy Schools Survey* (for certificated/professional staff)—provides research-based measures of school climate and organizational health.

Index

Subscriptions at a Glance

ERS

If you are looking for reliable preK-12 research to . . .

- tackle the challenges of NCLB;
- identify research-based teaching practices;
- make educationally sound and cost-effective decisions; and most importantly
- improve student achievement . . .

then look no further than an ERS Subscription.

Simply pick the subscription option that best meets your needs:

■ **School District Subscription**—a special research and information subscription that provides education leaders with timely research on priority issues in preK-12 education. All new ERS publications and periodicals, access to customized information services through the ERS special library, and 50 percent discounts on additional ERS resources are included in this subscription for one annual fee. This subscription also provides the entire administrative staff "instant" online, searchable access to the wide variety of ERS resources. You'll gain access to the ERS electronic library of more than 1,600 educational research-based documents, as well as additional content uploaded throughout the year.

■ **Individual Subscription**—designed primarily for school administrators, staff, and school board members who want to receive a personal copy of new ERS studies, reports, and/or periodicals published and special discounts on other resources purchased.

■ **Other Education Agency Subscription**—available for state associations, libraries, departments of education, service centers, and other organizations needing access to quality research and information resources and services.

Your ERS Subscription benefits begin as soon as your order is received and continue for 12 months. For more detailed subscription information and pricing, contact ERS toll free at 800-791-9308, by email at ers@ers.org, or visit us online at www.ers.org!

ERS ORDER FORM FOR RELATED RESOURCES

Quantity	Item Number	Title	Base Price	ERS Individual Subscriber Discount Price	ERS School District Subscriber Discount Price	Total Price
				Price per Item		
	0711	*How to Conduct Survey Research: A Guide for Schools*	$28.00	$21.00	$14.00	
	0496	*Understanding Education Statistics: It's Easier (and More Important) Than You Think, Second Edition*	$20.00	$15.00	$10.00	
	0538	*Handbook of Research on Improving Student Achievement, 3rd Edition*	$44.00	$33.00	$22.00	
	0423	*The Informed Educator: Using Assessment Data to Improve Instruction*	$9.60	$7.20	$4.80	
		Shipping and Handling** (Add the greater of $4.50 or 10% of purchase price.)				
		Express Delivery** (Add $20 for second-business-day service.)				
		**Please double for international orders.			TOTAL PRICE:	

SATISFACTION GUARANTEED! If you are not satisfied with an ERS resource, return it in its original condition within 30 days of receipt and we will give you a full refund.

Visit us online at www.ers.org for a complete listing of resources!

Method of payment:

☐ Check enclosed (payable to ERS)   ☐ P.O. enclosed (Purchase order #_____)

☐ MasterCard   ☐ VISA   ☐ American Express

Name on Card: _____ Credit Card #:_____

Expiration Date: _____ Signature: _____

Ship to: (please print or type)   ☐ Dr.   ☐ Mr.   ☐ Mrs.   ☐ Ms.

Name:_____ Position: _____

School District or Agency: _____ ERS Subscriber ID#: _____

Street Address:_____

City, State, Zip: _____

Telephone: _____ Fax: _____

Email: _____

Return completed order form to:
Educational Research Service • 1001 North Fairfax Street, Suite 500 • Alexandria, VA 22314-1587
Phone: 703-243-2100 • Toll Free Phone: 800-791-9308 • Fax: 703-243-1985 • Toll Free Fax: 800-791-9309
Email: ers@ers.org • Web site: www.ers.org